D1271589

Dieter Roth   96 Piccadillies

Dieter Roth

96 Piccadillies

Eaton House Publishers Ltd

published 1977 by edition hansjörg mayer   stuttgart   london
first edition 2000 copies   of which 200 de luxe
(half each for eaton house publishers ltd   with an
introduction by dieter schwarz)
printed in germany
© coypright 1977   dieter roth   zug
© copyright introduction 1977   dieter schwarz   zürich

content

Vorwort
Foreword

Um den Briefverkehr mir zu erleichtern, dieweil das Malen und Zeichnen mir leichter fällt als das Denken und Schreiben, übermale ich d. r. seit einem Vierteljahrhundert Postkarten, dieweil das Malen und Zeichnen auf unbemaltem oder unbezeichnetem Papier schwerer fällt als auf Papier, wo schan was drauf ist. Als er in England weilte bei seinem guten Freunde Richard und seiner bensoguten Freundin Rita müsste es gewesen sein dass er jene Postkarten sichtete die man die Piccadilly Zirkus Postkarten nennt, sammelte doch Rita Donagh Piccadillies, nicht nur in Form der Postkarte sondern auch in Form vieles Anderen. Sollte es anders gewesen sein, so könnte er es heute am 1. September 1977, dem 28. Jahrestage des Beginns des entsetzlichen Krieges zwischen den entsetzlichen, mörde-

rischen Menschen, Deutsche, Engländer, Amerikaner, Russen, Franzosen, Italiener genannt, in folgender Form auf Papier erscheinen: Ich weis es nicht mehr. Im Jahre 1968 einige Monate in England lebend, schrieb er viele Briefe in Gestalt der bemalten Postkarte an Freund und Feind, dieweil das Böse, das sogenannte, in Form des Geschriebenen Wortes, nicht als Böses vom Leser in der Eigenschaft des Bösbreifempfängers nicht so stark kritisiert werden zu können scheint wenn ein buntes Bild auf der anderen, Rückseite genannten Seite lächeln zu dürfen die Aufforderung in wieweit es hier nicht mehr weitergeht, weiss D. R. nun nicht. Um des Leichten Geldes zu verdienen oder nicht zu verdienen, jedoch wenigstens zu erwerben, nehmen oder drübergelangen, schmiert er oft lange breite

flächen voll, so auch der Geschäftsmann zu gedacht haben er, De Er, sich denkt, glaubt er schreiben zu dürfen, jener, welcher kam, den Namen Paule trganed, auffordernd zu gewaltige Haufen Geldes, in imagination sich vorzustellen oder vorzulegen, zu welchem Ende, oder auch nur Zwischenstation vielleicht jedoch allein, man male auf Post-

kartengleiche Flächen mit den Motiven der Postkarte, für Engländer und wissend=kennede Turisten, Tourists, Piccadilly nicht zu nenn nötig zu werden erscheint dem hier schreibenden Zahnschmerz. Zur schnellen beförderung des von da=an zu befördernden, Gegseitig anstehend, abwartend farben und Gelder,

zeigte sich Wut schon, horizontererweise laut pfeidend
Lieder von Screenprint et ce tera et cetera et.
Stockt nun die Saga vom dem was gesagt werden sollt
wollt's nämlich nicht aufs Flachpier sich ergeben,
schaun wir ins Schwarzloch hinein, scheuernt er schwächlich zugleich,
zittert wien Rochen,
auf sich biegenden knochen
shaking like a hissing f
fisch while pissing,

does he look into it, called black hole etce, tera etcetera saying, pissing like fishmeat in holes, blacked in desparate ins'bordination,

the saga does not give itself to paper, nor to speedy transports of feeling the money coming. Rather painfully waiting for speedy

A

Erleichterung brieflichen Verkehrs
aus d. Vorwort zu »96 Piccadillies«, 1977
9/12 Sabon und Cornelia

Dieter Roth, Coll. Works, Vol. 36   96 Piccadillies   edition hj. mayer, stuttgart, london

B

the saga does not give itself to paper
fr. the foreword to "96 Piccadillies", 1977
9/12 Cornelia

Dieter Roth, Coll. Works, Vol. 36   96 Piccadillies   edition hj. mayer, stuttgart, london

transports of money and Paintings or prints, he toothache cased in, living a life far from Tourists and their centers, like Piccadillies, stations of fear, to be too far from comfort and other ends at the other end of life, where tourists linger, each a golden Ring on his, her or it's finger. Now Paul Cornwall comes into the pisture, stepping on to the page letterwise, telling the tale of painty sprinkle, a version of the tall tale of purpose and future, stepping in on this page porpoisewise, wise as a turtle, Turtle steps out now and in comes, into a horrible war of bloody butchering bad, mad daddies, shit on shovel, Germans, Americans, English, etc al., werde deutsche Sprach versteh, der das da oben les ka, back in time only thoughts can run, slide, ride and hide, and on the wings of thought we he, di Dietrich, wnaders in wonder, arriving, far far in his, and others' past, what one colls or calls, his far past, not too far away, htough, to be inspected as close as a can of beer could be, and there he says, i say, where are we? – Who we? – Herr Ichweissnicht und Madame Duweissnicht! – and they sing the song of canned beer, going thus:

So wie das Fleisch in Fischen singt und webet,
so wohl der Mensch, hinaus ins Wasser strebend,
sich wohl ersäuft in Alkoholes Postkart Meer,
sendet die Grüsse tief ausm Wassr er her,
Gut acht, haut ab, ihr dummen Schweine, allgemein,
balbli blabla, soll unsre Losung sein.
As if a fish is lifting his tall stein,
so man is lifting water with combine,

of cans of beer and alcohol to boot,
still sending greetinges from cadaques, aloof
of watermelon butterball shitcan and other loot,
hoot, hoot, pervade, stay put, hootoot!

Thus going, canned beer singing a song of, they sing: Herr i do not know, who are we, and: say, could that be there a can of beer? – Where? There, where that can of be seems to be allowed to behave like a tumbler of wine. Closely inspected though, it calls for others' past, not far away, rider of horse slides into the gorse pile his bucket full of remorese. Those are the sounds of mad Daddie mammy, only to ease my life's rising pain and to ease the duty of answering letters, since painting and drawing falls easier into my Hands than thoughtful writing, i paint, a quarter of a centruy might have passed my idontknowwhat, on postcards. Ersatz-letters of ease, since painting on empty paper would have to be called youknowwhat, namely paper on which there is nothing yet. When D. R. (Karl-Dietrich the Timid) whaling a while in England, cooly cruel Geearbee, with his good friend Richard and as well his good friend Rita, collecter of piccadilly postcards, it must be something to say now, namely he did find etc et al. Should it habe been otherwise going, he could not well, today, on the 28th anniversary of that awful butcheries beginning, ahich involved butchers from Germany, England Northamerica, France and Italy as well as the rest, bewriting the name of it: Hellish war, by Russians Germans and Englishmen, fucking away like mastadons of old, but he does not know anymore, life has confused him,

C

Grüsse aus der Tiefe des Wassers
aus d. Vorwort zu »96 Piccadillies«, 1977
9/12 Cornelia

Dieter Roth, Coll. Works, Vol. 36   96 Piccadillies   edition hj. mayer, stuttgart, london

---

D

Butchering English, Germans et al
fr. the foreword to "96 Piccadillies", 1977
9/12 Cornelia

Dieter Roth, Coll. Works, Vol. 36   96 Piccadillies   edition hj. mayer, stuttgart, london

painting postcards to friends and enemies confusingly thinking of them, writing many letters in the shape of bitter ducks, or swans or moscitos, stinging the stingy, but now he does not know for the second time how it all etc. But, Paul, eater of future, kicker of past, steps in, smiling like the front of a painted postcard we all like to see each other, living for three month space of time in London, England. Simply to make gain shovel money, he fills often and strenching awfully in time, lengthwise, he does not now know. To make easy money, he thinks himself beeing allowed to write, there P. coming on widthwise thinking long letters, but he himself painting big things, pst card like, like heps or heaps of spells of mountains of regret, or fretfully small stations on lifes dusty rusty road to hell. Musty waffles. He came, bearing his name to the fore, asking from D. R. mighty efforts, gaining streches of lost time forever, tickling the seconds minutes and hours towards the end, where pisty Pastures for youknowwhat stand by, itching for more, singing

counterclockwise, beheaded, count Clock wisely heads for the doorbell,
sticking a bending bone deepl'into Bell Door's teat.
Is now the question wether, he well first is or she is,
in giving way to you know what i W's going to say
lettering on on this letterheads heapful of hyperoporo.
Rocklike shaking
always waking
in the way of wake of stars and moons,

always caking,
cakes abaking
shaking as sticking in pudding spoons.
Flach wie Flundern
vom sich über Postkarten wundern
dumm wie Sonne Mond und Stern,
heiss wie Kacke,
kalt wie Schlacke,
folgt die Poka ihrem Stern.
Pisst der Fisch
und schaut hinein in das schwarz genannte Loch,
undsoweiter undsoweiter sagt er sagt er sagt er doch

nicht, sondern schwarze verdammte, verwegene Aufbegehrung hält die Geschichte, und die gibt sich dem Liegen auf Papier nicht hin, noch dem schmerzlichen Warten auf Ladungen Gefühls von kommendem Gelde her. Eher schmerzlich wartend auf schnelle Transporte Geldes und Gemälde oder Drucke, er Zahnschmerz einfasste, ein Leben weit entfernt von Turisten und ihren Zentern lebend. Wie Pickeldille, Haltestellen der Angst, zu weit vom Bequemen entfernt zu sein und anderen Zwecken am anderen Ende des Lebens, wo Turisten warten, jeder einen goldenen Ring an seinem, ihrem oder seinem Finger. Da kommt Paul Kornwand ins Bild, buchstabenweislich auf die Seite in die Seite tretend, die Geschichte von Male Spritzer erzählend,

E
confusing friends and enemies
fr. the foreword to "96 Piccadillies", 1977
9/12 Cornelia

Dieter Roth, Coll. Works, Vol. 36   96 Piccadillies   edition hj. mayer, stuttgart, london

F
Pissing Fish
fr. the foreword to "96 Piccadillies", 1977
9/12 Cornelia

Dieter Roth, Coll. Works, Vol. 36   96 Piccadillies   edition hj. mayer, stuttgart, london

eine Version der Geschichte grossartigen von Unternehmensentschiedenheit und Zukunft, In der Weise der Kröte herein auf diese Seite tretend, Wie ne Kröte so weise, tritt Kröte nun hervor und hereinkommt, nachdem Schildkröte o.k., in einen erschrecklich horiblen Krieg von bltutiglich schlachtender Schlechtigkeit, verreckte, verrückte Racker, den Scheiss auf ihrer Schaufel, Deutsche, Schweizer, Amerikaner, Engländer u.a.m., he hoo etc etc etc. der kann das da oben etc. zurü in die Zeit nur Gedanken rennen können, gleiten, reiten, verbeiten, und auf den Schwingen des Denkens wir ihn, de Dietrich, sich wundernd wandernd, ankommend, weit weit in seiner, und anderer, Vergangenheit, was man nännt oder nennt, seine weit entfernte Vergangenheit, jedoch nicht zu weit entfernt, aus der Nähe betrachten wie eine Bierkanne man könnte, und dann sagt er, sag ichs, wo sind wir? – Wer wir? – Mr. Idonotknow and Madame Youdonotknow! – Und sie singen den Sang vom eingekannten Bier, der sich so anhört:

So well as flesh, called meat sings inside fish and wavers,
so man well also, swinging seaward 's shavers,
well drowns in alcoholic depth on postcard small,
and all the greetings drown with it, and all
you pigs and pork, fare well, pile off the wall.
Blablablabla blabla, so we say all,
und da erhebt Herr Fisch den Krug,
wie man unter der Kombinaison ihn trug,
zur Zeit gekannten Biers mit alkohol darin,

noch immer sendend Grüsse her und hin,
greetings from Cadaques heist unser Wort
der Wörter, Wort der Wörter heisset unser Wort.

Gehend derart weiter, Bier in Kanne, singend den Gesang vom Singensie: Lord, ich weiss nicht, wer sind wir, und: sage, kann dort das sein eine Kanne Bier? – Woda? Dorten, dort wo die Kanne Bier in Erlaubnis sich zu bewegen scheint wie ein Weinkrug sich zu behnehmen, jedoch von nahem betrachtet. Es ruft nach anderer Leute Vergangenheit, nicht weit entfernt, Pferdereiter schlüpft in ins Kraut der Heide mit einem Eimer voll Leide. So tönt es aus Vattis Munde, Mammie!
Die Pflicht des Briefeschreibens zu erleichtern, da Zeichnen und Malen oder so leichter mir in meine Hände fällt als denkendes Schreiben, male ich, ein Viertel eines jahrhunderts mag vorbeigegangen sein an meinem Ichweissnichtwas, auf Postkarten. Ersatzbriefersatz von Leichtigkeit, da auf leeres Papier zu malen genannt werden müsste ihrwisstschonwas, nämlich Papier auf dem noch nichts drauf ist. Wenn D. R! (Karl-Dietrich der Ängstliche, walend eine Weile in England, Kühlgrausames GrB, mit seinem guten Freund Richard sowohl als auch seiner guten Freundin Rita, Sammlerin der Postkarten Pikkadillies, das muss etwas zu sagen sein jetzt, nämlich er tat finden etc uam. Sollte es gewesensein so dass andererart es ging, konnte er nicht gut, heuet, am 28. Jahrestag (heute schon Gestern) des Beginns jener fürchterlichen Schlachterei, mit Schlachtern aus Deutschland England, Nordamerika, Frankreich und Italien sowohl als auch destes Rest, anschreibend den Namen dessen: Höllischer Krieg, mit Russen,

G
auf den Schwingen des Denkens
aus d. Vorwort zu »96 Piccadillies«, 1977
9/12 Cornelia

Dieter Roth, Coll. Works, Vol. 36   96 Piccadillies   edition hj. mayer, stuttgart, london

H
Menschenschlachter
aus d. Vorwort zu »96 Piccadillies«, 1977
9/12 Cornelia

Dieter Roth, Coll. Works, Vol. 36   96 Piccadillies   edition hj. mayer, stuttgart, london

Deutschen und Engländern, losfickend wie uralte Mastodons, aber er weiss nicht mehr, das Leben hat ihn konfusioniert, im Postkartenschreiben an Freunde und Feinde, konfusionierterweise an sie denkend, viele Briefe in Gestalt bitterer Enten schreibend, oder Schwäne und Mücken, stechend den Geizigen, aber nun weiss er nimmermehr zum zweiten Male wie es alles etc. Aber, Paul, der Zukunftsfresser, Treter der Vergangenheit, tritt herein, lächelnd wie die Vorderseite einer gemalten Postkarte die wir alle zu sehen lieben einander, lebend in London während der Zeitdauer einner von 3 Monaten, England. Einfacherweise um Geld an die Schaufel zu tun, füllt er oft lange Strecken an Zeit, der Länge nach, er weiss es nicht. Leichtes Gekd zu machen, denkt er sich selber erlaubt zu schreiben, dort Paul kommt, breiterweise lange Briefe denkend, aber er selber malend Grosse Dinger, wie Postkarten, wie Häufen oder Haufen von Bannmeilen von Bergen des Bedauerns, oder schrechartiglich stinkende, nein, stehende stationen an des Lebens Wegen, andes Lebens Rostroten Wegen zur Hölle. Schimmelnde Waffeln. Er kam, seinen Namen in den Vordergrund bringend, fragend nach mächtigen Anstrengungen von D. R's Seite, gewinnende Strecken an Zeit, für immer verlorene, die Sekunden, Minuten und Stunden auf das Ende zu kitzelnd, dort wo Biffe Bilder wartend auf ihrwisstwas stehend, nach mehr sich umkratzend, singend weilen, singend:

Gegen die Uhrzeigerrichtung den Kopf zu senken der Weise
brauchet nicht da er den Knopf biegenden Knochens versenkt
in der Titte der Belle drin. Fragt man aber nun wer ists
der hier als erstes gibt nach, er oder sie oder er?

Oder auch sie kann den Brief nur vollenden als Poka.
zittern wien Fels
witternd wien Wels,
auf die Weise der sterne und Monde,
noch ein klein schnell
Hundegebell
zitternd wien Hundekuchen im Mond.
Flat as Flounders,
from postcards bounding,
stupid as sun, moon and star,
hot as turdy,
cold and sturdy,
shouting like a star.
Pissis fish in holed up Black and so on and so on he

says bravely he says bravely not yet, but black, condemned insurrecton insurrection, rechlessly keeps the story, and it does not give itself to lying on paper, nor to the painful waiting for loads of feeling from Money far away, coming money. Rather painfully waiting for speedy deliveries of money, paintings or prints, he encompassed toothache for about the length of a life distant from tourists and their centers living. As Piccadilly, stations of fear, to be stationed too far from stations of comfort and other goals at the other end of life, where tourists aere waiting, each a golden ring

I

Alte Mastodone
aus d. Vorwort zu »96 Piccadillies«, 1977
9/12 Cornelia

Dieter Roth, Coll. Works, Vol. 36   96 Piccadillies   edition hj. mayer, stuttgart, london

J

Faraway Money
fr. the foreword to "96 Piccadillies", 1977
9/12 Cornelia

Dieter Roth, Coll. Works, Vol. 36   96 Piccadillies   edition hj. mayer, stuttgart, london

around his hers or its finger. There, Paul Cornwall is stepping into the picture, letterwise or letterwisely into the side on the side, telling the story of Paint Spritzer, another version of the big tale of undertakers' elegance and spree in the future, White as a turtle, porpoise is stepping in now and comes on and steps in, after porpoise has been okeyd. In an horrible war of bloody badness, dying, bad, crazy reckletters, everybody like Swiss, Germans, Russians Hessians and English with French and Italien, there he cans it, back in time to rush he can, riding, sliding, asiding, and on the wingws of thought we see him, von Dietrich der Trügerische Wiesel, wonderously wandering, arriving, far, far away, in his own and other past, what one cells or calls, his far distanced past, but not too distanced, but to be inspected from nearby close like a can of beer under ones nose, and then he says and i say, where are we? – who we? – Herr Ichweissnicht und Frau Duweissesnicht! – And they sing the song of canned, it sounds like this:

So gut wie'm Fleisch s'im Fisch auch innen singet,
so dringt Mann ein, schwingend ein Schwert, geklinget
mit alkoholes Schärfe, Kehlen wüst und leer und leer
zerschneidend, sägend hin und hin und hin und her,
das schmerzt so sehr soso sehr sehr sososo mehr her.
Sagen wir einmal bla bla, so sagen wir bla bla bla immer,
lifteth, my Fish, thou, your can now, the inhold gets slimmer.
And there, Heinz Fisch lifts hoch his stein,
as many a girl lifts hoch das Bein,

as many men lift to their mouthes can
that what so full of beer that one has to call it beer-can.

Greetings from Cadaques.
Walking, beer in can, singing the song of Lord: i do not know whats going on on earth, he says: Say, Herr, is that there a beercan? - wherethere? - Therethere, where that little beercan for permission to ask seems to behave like a tumbler of wine, looked at closely, thpugh. It calls for other peoples past, though, not far away, horses rider slips, on gorse-cider: CRACK ! so it sounds out of Pappa's mouth, Mamma! But Mamma hassich abgewendet und schraubt uns den Arschberg auf den Horizont, ein Vulkan tost erbost, Geschrei wird vernommen: Heh, um den Briefverkehr macht Euch die Zeit nicht lang, den erleichtern sie sich mit Pokas, die weil Malen und Schmieren leicht fällt, wie Denken und Schreiben. Übermalt, seid ihr einer Vierteljahrhundert = Postkarte, dieweil Malen, Schmieren und Zeichnen aufsmal schwerer fällt als Papier, worauf, als er in England weilte, fielen: Sein guter Freund und seine ebensogute Freundin, die müssten es gewesen sein, welche jene Postkarten sichteten, welche man die Piccadilly = Zirkuspostkarten nennt. Sammelten doch Reiter sich am Pcy. Zks., nicht nur in Form der Pferdearten sondern auch inform vieles Anderen. Sollte es gewesen sein? Ach, könnte er heute, am 2. September 1977, dem 28. Jahrestage des Beginns jenes entsetzlichen Krieges zwischen den folgenden M.= M.'s A. 'n: Deutsche, Engländer, Amerikaner, Russen, Frabzosen, Ytaliener, u. a. m., inform einer Folge auf Papier erscheinen, ich weiss nicht, ob er mehr als einige Monate in England leben täte, schrieb er doch viel an Briefen (in Gestalt Form=bemalter

K
Leglifting Girls
fr. the foreword to "96 Piccadillies", 1977
9/12 Cornelia

Dieter Roth, Coll. Works, Vol. 36   96 Piccadillies   edition hj. mayer, stuttgart, london

L
schwieriges Denken und Schreiben
aus d. Vorwort zu »96 Piccadillies«, 1977
9/12 Cornelia und Sabon

Dieter Roth, Coll. Works, Vol. 36   96 Piccadillies   edition hj. mayer, stuttgart, london

Pokaster) an Freund, Feind und Freund; Böses inform geschriebener Worte, nicht als böse Leser in der Eigenschaft des Rattenfängers, sondern nicht so stark irigiert werden zu können, scheint, wenn ein buntes Bild auch, so doch auf der anderen, der Rückseite. Dieser Seite lächeln zu dürfen, eine Aufforderung, zu sagen in wie weit es hier nicht mehr weitergehe, weiss D. R. sich nicht Erlaubnis=fähig. Um des leichten Geldverdienens oder =nichtverdienens willen erwarb wenigstens er dies: Zu nehmen oder drüberzugelangen, schmiert er oft lange, beite Flächen voll, so der Geschäftsmann.

Es gedacht zu haben, ES, dem er, sich denkend, glaubt zuschreiben zu dürfen – als jenen, welcher kam, den Namen Paul zu tragen – auffordernd zu gewaltige Haufen Geldes imaginationieren, sich auch vorzustellen oder vorzulegen, zu dem Ende oder nur Zwischenstation, jedoch allein, allein. Man malt auf Postkarten nicht. Man hat Flächen mit den Motiven der Pokarte, für Egländer und wissentlich kennende Turisten »Tourists« zu nenn' nicht nötig, erscheint dem hier Schreibenden. Zahnschmerz, zur schnellen Förderung des zu Fördernden stehend, wartet Farben und Gelder.

Geigt sich Wut schon, hinterm Horizonte pfeiffend,
Lieder von dem Skreenprint, et ce t'ra,
stockt die Sag' von dem was g'sagt werd' sollte,
denn aufs Papier ergeben es nicht sich wollte.
Schaun wir ins Schwarze hinein, gemächlich es scheuert,
wie ein zitternder Knochen
im sich biegenden Rochen,

shaking a hissing fart
out of Herr Fishes, while, of pissing,
Feeshe looks into the black hole, saying:

Hissing like wholesale fishmeat, bakedly and desparately, ordination wins the saga. Does not it itself give in to power, nor on to those speedy transports of feeling, that money makes come. Painfully waiting for speed, money, paintings or prints, the toothache ceased to live a life far from the tourists' center. It likes Pickle Dill's stations of fear, far from comfort, at the (other) end of life, where tubists linger, each (of them) a gilded ring on finger. Now, Paul, Cornwall comes in to the pisture! stepting on to the poge. Now, D. R., tell the tale of painty sprinkle! a version of tall of the tale of old

or porpoise und fouture, stepping on to this page purposewise, as porpoises do, like wise. Since wise is the turtle that steps out. How in the end come, into a war of Butchers, bad Madaddies, shit onshovel, Dermans, Amoricons, Oglish, et all others. Wer die Deutsche Spreche versteht, der kann das da oben lesen. Back in time, thoughts can run, slide, ride and hide, and on the wings of sorrow we Dietrichs, wander in wonder, arriving, though not thinking far, in his, this and the others' past, what one calls or calle, this far past, not too far away, though, not to be inspected closely, as close as a can of beer can be. It says:

    – Say, where are we?
    – Who, we?
    – Herr Ichweissnicht and Mrs. Duweisstnicht.

M
Wut geigt und pfeifft
aus d. Vorwort zu »96 Piccadillies«, 1977
9/12 Sabon

Dieter Roth, Coll. Works, Vol. 36   96 Piccadillies   edition hj. mayer, stuttgart, london

N
Dermans and Amoricons
fr. the foreword to "96 Piccadillies", 1977
9/12 Sabon

Dieter Roth, Coll. Works, Vol. 36   96 Piccadillies   edition hj. mayer, stuttgart, london

(They sing the song of old of canned beef:)
– So wie das Fleisch in Fisches Singen webt,
  so auch der Mensch heraus aus 'm Wasser strebt,
  sich zu ergehn an buntgedruckter Postkart' Strand,
  streckt seinen Kopf aus tiefem Wasser in den Sand,
  Streck wach, Haub Acht! Ihr Peine, A. Z. klein,
  Lalli – lalla! loll lunsre losung lein.
  As well as fishes, lifting their stein,
  betrayed, are lifting water in combine,
we, cans of beer and water, aquiline combustion,
sending greetings from Cadaqués,
  Butterball Shitcan was here!

Pervade, Butter! Stay put, force, being going,   canned Ball, sing force the song of old like:

  – I do not know who we are, Butt, say, could that there be a can of beer?
  – Where?

And there, where that can of beer seems to be allowed to be astumbling over a can of wine of old, in other words: Beer, closely inspected, though, calls for other pasts, not a far way, and rides horses' slides, the gorse's piles. Packets full of Remorese fall from those horses, making mad Dackels' sounds, like:

  – Wau, wau! the duty! – letters, writing letters, I presume ? ! –

Yeah, painting and drawing hand thoughtful writting over to a hand full of gorse on horses riding over the duty of writing (letters), but I paint, in a quarter of a night where my idontknowwhats have pissed, on postcards, letters of ease and ersatz, since painting on empty paper would, as you know, have to be called youknowwhat, like paper whereupon is nothing.
When Charles-Derdick the Timid with his cod food rich art and as well his friend foot rider, collectress of past cords, »It must be she!« something it was to say now, namely, when he did find Herrn Et Threthal. Should it have been otherwise going? He could not well tell, today, on the 28th anniv. of the Bloodies, which involved putchers from Ferbaly, Ebgland or Thame Rica, Prance and Staly, as well as the rest, called by the names of Hussians, Turtans and Eng Suc Ing, awaysliding Mastodons of old. Put their shoes not away anymore! life has them, postcards to friends and enemies, thinking of them confusingly, writing many letters in the shapes of bitter ducks and swans. Moscitos, swinging stingily their bitter ways, now for the second time, how come, it all . . . but Paul, Butt, eater of future, sticker of past, steps in, snidingly like the front of a painting. Cards, all alike, seep eachother, living in front of the mouth of space of old in time through London in England. Simply to make or gain shovel-money, he often fills and almost always streches awful spots of time. Lengthwise not now, though. Easy money to make, he himself writes too, there to P.Ow, coming on widthwise, thinking long lines of letters of old, but he is himself, painting big things of old, postcardwise, like heaps or mountains os regret, or fists-

O
Canned Beef
fr. the foreword to "96 Piccadillies", 1977
9/12 Sabon

Dieter Roth, Coll. Works, Vol. 36   96 Piccadillies   edition hj. mayer, stuttgart, london

P
the mouth of space
fr. the foreword to "96 Piccadillies", 1977
9/12 Sabon

Dieter Roth, Coll. Works, Vol. 36   96 Piccadillies   edition hj. mayer, stuttgart, london

fuls of stations of smallnesses of life on dusty rusty roads to – – hell! now i have forgotten where to!

Musty Waffles came, bearing his name wilfully, for the asking, from D. R. the Pile, of mighty efforts of becoming stretches of gaining lost time, forever, tickling seconds, minutes, hours and days to the end, after months and years, when Patsy Pastores for youknowwhat stands, singing:

Bound and blockwise bedded
Count Cock, wisely headed,
sticks his bone int' Bending Belle.
And it is the question, wether
first is well or second bether?
in giving way to weknowwhat –
lettering heapfuls of hyphons,
rocklike shaking,
high and waking,
in the ways of waterfalls,
always shaking
always high and farting,
in the ways of cannonballs,

thicking, as bakers do, in pulling pudding spare spats, flat as flounders, flach wie Flundern, von dem sich über beugenden Bäumen und vom sich über Postkarten Wundern und

vom über Bäumen sich Neigen und, krumm von Sonne, Mond und Stern, und die Berge in der Ferne sind heiss wie Kacke an dem Stocke, wie Zwerge, hockend in der Kacke, kalt wie Schlacke in der Socke. Wie Zwerge in den Bergen hockend, äugt die Pokastkarte ihren Stern, zeigt etc usw., isst der Fisch den usw. und schaut hinein in das schwarze Loch. Das Schwarze und das verwegenen Aufbegehren, die halten die Geschichte, die dem Liegen auf Papier nicht gibt sich hin, noch dem schmerzenden Warten auf geballte Gefühlsladungen, von kommendem Gelde her ausstrahlend. Den schmerzlich erwarteten Schnelltransport Geldes, Gemäldedrucke, Zahnschmerzeinfassungen, ein langes Leben weit entfernt von Turisten und ihren Zentnern. Wie Pickeldille, Haltestellen der Angst, tot wie eine Pickelgurke, weit vom Bequemen entfernt zu sein, und anderen Zwecken dienend gehorchen, am anderen Ende des Lebens, wo Turisten warten, jeder einen Ring am Finger aus Gold und Silber, wie Mond und Sterne, wie gesagt schon, anderen Zwecken als denen Sauls zu bequemlich dienen, wie zum Beispiel die Wand ins Bild fällt, Buchstaben – weise auf die Seite oder in die Seite tretend, aber zu dienen, die Geschichte von Maler Spritzer erzählen, in einer Version grossartigen, von Unternehmungsentschiedenheit und Fuhrwarenentschlossenheit überschäumenden Zukunftsgedankens, in der Weise der Kröten in die Seite des Bildes hereintretend, wie eine Kröte, so weise. So tritt Kröte nun hervor, und kommt herein, nachdem Schildkröte in einen schrecklich horribilen Krieg, von blutiglich schallendem Schlachten, Schlachtensmark und =bein erschallt. Verrückte Racker, den Scheiss auf ihrer Schaufel, Deutsche, Amerikaner Engländer, Russen, Polen und andere, u.a.m. heiho, etc. etc., der kann das da oben etc.! Zurück in die Zeit: Dass nur Gedanken dahin rennen können, das kön-

Q
Count Cannon on the Rocks
fr. the foreword to "96 Piccadillies", 1977
9/12 Sabon

Dieter Roth, Coll. Works, Vol. 36   96 Piccadillies   edition hj. mayer, stuttgart, london

R
Gemäldedrucke vom Krieg
aus d. Vorwort zu »96 Piccadillies«, 1977
9/12 Sabon

Dieter Roth, Coll. Works, Vol. 36   96 Piccadillies   edition hj. mayer, stuttgart, london

nen nur Worte sagen. Sieh, sie gleiten, reiten, verbreiten sich, verwundern, wie die Flundern, auf den Schwingen des Denkens, Neptuns Frohe Schar. Und wir greifen ihn, Dietrich den Schweiger, Friedrich das Pinsel, sich wundernd wandernd durch Berg und Tal, ankommend schliesslich in seiner – und anderer – Vergangenheit (sagt er), was man so nennt, jo, seine weit weit weit entfernte Vergangenheit. Jedoch nicht zu weit entfernt, ZU weit entfernt, sondern aus der Nähe, und IN der Nähe gesehen wie eine Bierkanne man sehen könnte oder sehen tut. Dann sagt er: Sagt' ichs nicht – wo sind wir?

Wir fragen entgegen: Wer, wir?

Er sagt: Mister I-Do-Not-Know plus Mistress You-Do-Not-Know. Und dann singen wir alle zusammen den Liedergesang vom eingemachten Bier, eingekannt manchmal genannt, welcher nämlicherweise sich folgendermaßen anhört:

As well as flesh, called meat, sings insides fish and weavers,
is man in fishes singing loud and beavers,
swinging his wavers seaward high and postcards small,
where all his greetings drown with him, so tall
and pork, as pigs pile from the wall.
Blablablablablablablablablablablablablabla,
so we say all.
No, so we do NOT say all!
Yes, so we say all!
Und da erhebt Herr Fisch den Krug,

den er unter dem Schuppenkombinaison trug,
und schüttet aus der Kanne Bier darein,
schwenkt ihn und taucht ne Poka rein:
»Greetings from Cadaques« heisst drauf das Wort,
das Wort der Wörter heisst es, dieses Wort an anderm Ort.

Dort geht er weiter, Dickrich die Selbstmäste, Bier in Kanne, singend.

Blablablabla blabla, so we say all,
und da erhebt Herr Fisch den Krug,
wie man unter der Kombinaison ihn trug,
zur Zeit eingekannten Biers mit Alkohol darin,
noch immer sendend Grüsse her und hin,
greetings from Cadaques! heisst unser Wort
der Wörter, Wort der Wörter! heisset unser Wort!

Gehend weiter, Bier in Kanne, singend den Gesang vom Singen: Lord, ich weiss nicht, wer sind wir? und: Sage, kann, dort das, sein eine Kanne Bier? – Woda? – Dorten, wo die Kanne Bier in Erlaubnis sich zu bewegen scheint ein Weinkrug zu sein, jedoch, von Nahem gehört, ruft sie nach anderer Leute Vergangenheit, nicht weit entfernt, Pferdereiter schlüpft in ins Kraut der Heide mit einem Eimer voll Leide. So tönt es aus Vattis Munde, Mammie! Ja Vatti, so tönts aus Mammas Crack! Der Pflicht des Briefe-

S
Wer sind wir?
aus d. Vorwort zu »96 Piccadillies«, 1977
9/12 Sabon

Dieter Roth, Coll. Works, Vol. 36   96 Piccadillies   edition hj. mayer, stuttgart, london

T
Dickrich die Selbstmühle
aus d. Vorwort zu »96 Piccadillies«, 1977
9/12 Sabon

Dieter Roth, Coll. Works, Vol. 36   96 Piccadillies   edition hj. mayer, stuttgart, london

schreibens eins zu erleichtern, da Zeichnen und Malen oder so leichter ihr in die Hände fällt als denkendes Schreiben, male ich, ein Viertel eines jahrhunderts mag vorbeigegangen sein an meinem Ichweissnichtwas, auf Postkarten. Ersatzbriefersatz von Leichtigkeit, da auf leeres Papier zu malen genannt werden müsste ihrwisstschonwas, nämlich Papier auf dem noch nichts drauf ist. Wenn D. R! (Karl-Dietrich der Ängstliche, walend eine Weile in England, Kühlgrausames GrB, mit seinem guten Freund Richard sowohl als auch seiner guten Freundin Rita, Sammlerin der Postkarten Pikkadillies, das muss etwas zu sagen sein jetzt, nämlich er tat finden etc. uam. Sollte es gewesensein so dass andererart es ging, konnte er nicht gut, heuet, am 28. Jahrestag (heute schon Gestern) des Beginns jener fürchterlichen Schlachterei, mit Schlachtern aus Deutschland England, Nordamerika, Frankreich und Italien sowohl als auch destes

Rest, anschreibend den Namen dessen: Höllischer Krieg, mit Russen, Deutschen und Engländern, losfickend wie uralte Mastodons, aber er weiss nicht mehr, das Leben hat ihn konfusioniert, im Postkartenschreiben an Freunde und Feinde, konfusionierterweise an sie denkend, viele Briefe in Gestalt bitterer Enten schreibend, oder Schwäne und Mücken, stechend den Geizigen, aber nun weiss er nimmermehr zum zweiten Male wie es alles etc. Aber, Paul, der Zukunftsfresser, Treter der Vergangenheit, tritt herein, lächelnd wie die Vorderseite einer gemalten Postkarte die wir alle zu sehen lieben einander, lebend in London während der Zeitdauer einer von 3 Monaten, England. Einfacherweise um Geld an die Schaufel zu tun, füllt er oft lange Strecken an Zeit, der Länge nach, er weiss es nicht. Leichtes Geld zu machen, denkt er sich selbem erlaubt zu schreiben, dort Paul kommt, breiterweise lange Briefe denkend, aber er selber malend

Grosse Dinger, wie Postkarten, wie Häufen oder Haufen von Bannmeilen von Bergen des Bedauerns, oder schrechartiglich stinkende, nein, stehende stationen an des Lebens Wegen, andes Lebens Rostroten Wegen zur Hölle. Schimmelnde Waffeln. Er kam, seinen Namen in den Vordergrund bringend, fra-

gend nach mächtigen Anstrengungen von D. R's seite, gewinnende Strecke an Zeit, für immer verlorene, die Sekunden, Minuten und Studen auf das Ende zu kitzelnd, dort wo Biffe Bilder wartend auf ihrwisstwas stehend, nach mehr sich umkratzend, singend weilen, singend :

Gegen die Uhrzeigerrichtung den Kopf zu senken der Weise
brauchet nicht da er den Knopf biegenden Knochens versenkt
in der Titte der Belle drin. Fragt man aber nun wer ists
der hier als erstes gibt nach, er oder sie oder er?
Oder auch sie kann den Brief nur vollenden als Poka.
zitternd wien Fels
witternd wien Wels,
auf die Weise der sterne und Monde,
noch ein klein schnell
Hundegebell
zitternd wien Hundekuchen im Mond.
Flat as Flounders,
from postcards bounding,
stupid as sun, moon and star,

U

Konfusioniertes Postkartenschreiben
aus d. Vorwort zu »96 Piccadillies«, 1977
9/12 Sabon

Dieter Roth, Coll. Works, Vol. 36   96 Piccadillies   edition hj. mayer, stuttgart, london

---

V

Hundegebell im Mond und Grosse Dinger
aus d. Vorwort zu »96 Piccadillies«, 1977
9/12 Sabon und Cornelia

Dieter Roth, Coll. Works, Vol. 36   96 Piccadillies   edition hj. mayer, stuttgart, london

hot as turdy,
cold and sturdy,
shouting like a star.
Pisses fish in holed up Black and so on and so on he

says bravely he says bravely not yet, but black, condemned insurrecto insurrection, rechlessly keeps the story, and it does not give itself to lying on paper, nor to the painful waiting for loads of feeling from Money far away, coming money. Rather painfully waiting for speedy deliveries of money, paintings or prints, he encompassed toothache for about the length of a life distant from tourists and their center living. As Piccadilly, stations of fear, to be stationed too far from stations of comfort and other goals at the other end of life, where tourists aere waiting, each a golden ring araound his hers or its finger. There, Paul Cornwall is stepping into the picture, letterwise or letterwisely into the side on

the side, telling the story of Paint Spritzer, another version of the big tale of undertakers' elegance and spree in the future, White as a turtle, porpoise is stepp in now and comes on and steps in, after porpoise has been okeyd. In an horrible war of bloody badness, dying, bad, crazy reckletters, everybody like Swiss, Germans, Russians Hessians and English with French and Italien, there he cans it, back in time to rush he can, riding, sliding, asiding, and on the wingws of thought we see him von Dietrich der Trügerische Wiesel, wonderously wandering, arriving far, far away, in his own and other past, what one cells or calls, far distanced past, but not too distanced, but to be inspected from nearby close like

a con of beer under ones nose, and then he says and i say, where are we? – who we? –

Herr Ichweissnicht und Frau Duweissesnicht! – And they sing the song of canned, it sounds like this:

So gut wie'm Fleisch s'im Fisch auch innen singet,
  so dringt Mann ein, schwingend ein Schwert, geklinget
  mit Alkalides Schärfe, Kehlen wüst und leer und leer
  zerschneidend, sägend hin und hin und hin und her,
  das schmerzt so sehr soso sehr sehr sososo sehr mehr.
Sagen wir einmal hellblau, so sagen wir dunkelblau immer,
  lifteth, my Fish, thou, your can now, the inhold gets slimmer.
And there, Heinz Fisch lifts hoch his Stein,
  as many a Girl lifts hoch das Bein,
  as many Men lift to their mouthes Can
that what so full of Beer that one has to call it Beer-Can.

Greetings from Cadaques.
Walking, beer in can, singing the song of Lord, i do not know whats going on on earth, he says: Say, Herr, is that there a beercan? – wherethere? – Therethere, where that little beercan for permission to ask seems to behave like a tumbler of wine,

looked at closely, thpugh. It calls for other peoples' past. Though not far away, horses' rider slips into gorse cider, CRACK! so it sounds out of Mappa's mouth, Pamma! Mappa! Mouth Pamma's of out soundsit so BLACK !

D. R. Stuttgart, Sept. 77

W
at the other end of life
fr. the foreword to "96 Piccadillies", 1977
9/12 Cornelia

Dieter Roth, Coll. Works, Vol. 36   96 Piccadillies   edition hj. mayer, stuttgart, london

X
! Greetings From Cadaqués !
fr. the foreword to "96 Piccadillies", 1977
9/12 Cornelia

Dieter Roth, Coll. Works, Vol. 36   96 Piccadillies   edition hj. mayer, stuttgart, london

Piccadilly Circus, London.   (15)   *Photograph by John Hinde Studios*   D.R. 71.

1
Piccadilly Circus, London (ca. 1965)
Picture Postcard from a suite of 16, 1971
10 x 14 cm

Dieter Roth, Coll. Works, Vol. 36   96 Piccadillies   edition hj. mayer, stuttgart, london

2
Postcard to Rita Donagh, 1968
Acrylic on offsetprinting on card
9 x 13 cm

Dieter Roth, Coll. Works, Vol. 36   96 Piccadillies   edition hj. mayer, stuttgart, london

3

Base-print from '6 Piccadillies', 1969
Offsetprinting on card
50 x 70 cm

Dieter Roth, Coll. Works, Vol. 36   96 Piccadillies   edition hj. mayer, stuttgart, london

4

Base-print from '6 Piccadillies', 1969
Offsetprinting on card
50 x 70 cm

Dieter Roth, Coll. Works, Vol. 36   96 Piccadillies   edition hj. mayer, stuttgart, london

5

Study for '6 Piccadillies', 1969
Acrylic paint on offsetprinting on card on board
50 x 70 cm

Dieter Roth, Coll. Works, Vol. 36   96 Piccadillies   edition hj. mayer, stuttgart, london

6

Study for '6 Piccadillies', 1969
Glue on offsetprinting on card on board
50 x 70 cm

Dieter Roth, Coll. Works, Vol. 36   96 Piccadillies   edition hj. mayer, stuttgart, london

7
Study for '6 Piccadillies', 1969
Acrylic paint on screenprinting on offsetprinting
on card on board
50 x 70 cm

Dieter Roth, Coll. Works, Vol. 36   96 Piccadillies   edition hj. mayer, stuttgart, london

8
Study for '6 Piccadillies', 1969
Cocoa-powder on glue and acrylic paint
on offsetprinting on card on board
50 x 70 cm

Dieter Roth, Coll. Works, Vol. 36   96 Piccadillies   edition hj. mayer, stuttgart, london

9
Study for '6 Piccadillies', 1969
Cocoa-powder and acrylic paint on acetate
in transparent sleeve
50 x 70 cm

Dieter Roth, Coll. Works, Vol. 36   96 Piccadillies   edition hj. mayer, stuttgart, london

10
Giant Piccadilly, 1969–73
Chocolate, cocoa-powder and glue on photographic
colour print on canvas
160 x 220 cm

Dieter Roth, Coll. Works, Vol. 36   96 Piccadillies   edition hj. mayer, stuttgart, london

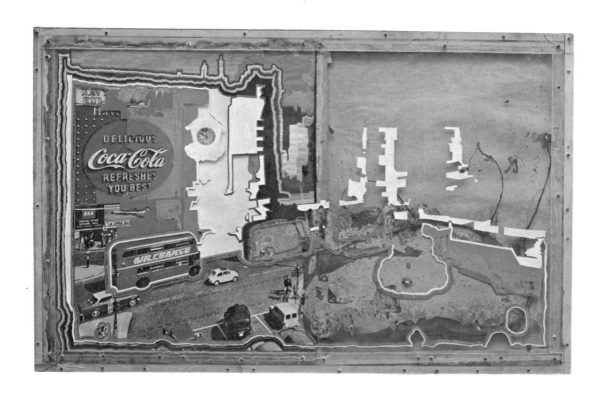

11
Giant Double-Piccadilly, 1969–73
one side
Chocolate, acrylic paint and/on photographic
colour print on canvas
160 x 220 cm

Dieter Roth, Coll. Works, Vol. 36   96 Piccadillies   edition hj. mayer, stuttgart, london

12
Giant Double-Piccadilly, 1969–73
other side
Chocolate, acrylic paint and/on photographic
colour print on canvas
160 x 220 cm

Dieter Roth, Coll. Works, Vol. 36   96 Piccadillies   edition hj. mayer, stuttgart, london

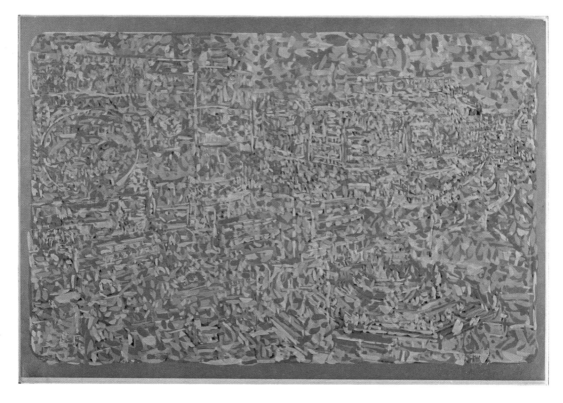

13
Singlecoloured print from '6 Piccadillies', 1969–70
Screenprinting on offsetprinting on card on board under
card under offsetprinting under screenprinting
50 x 70 cm

Dieter Roth, Coll. Works, Vol. 36   96 Piccadillies   edition hj. mayer, stuttgart, london

14
Spotty print from '6 Piccadillies', 1969–70
Screenprinting on offsetprinting on card on board under
card under offsetprinting under screenprinting
50 x 70 cm

Dieter Roth, Coll. Works, Vol. 36   96 Piccadillies   edition hj. mayer, stuttgart, london

15
Print with cracked surface from '6 Piccadillies', 1969–70
Screenprinting on offsetprinting on card on board under
card under offsetprinting under screenprinting
50 x 70 cm

Dieter Roth, Coll. Works, Vol. 36   96 Piccadillies   edition hj. mayer, stuttgart, london

16
Print with elevated surface from '6 Piccadillies', 1969–70
Screenprinting on offsetprinting on card on board under
card under offsetprinting under screenprinting
50 x 70 cm

Dieter Roth, Coll. Works, Vol. 36   96 Piccadillies   edition hj. mayer, stuttgart, london

17
Multicoloured print from '6 Piccadillies', 1969–70
Screenprinting on offsetprinting on card on board under
card under offsetprinting under screenprinting
50 x 70 cm

Dieter Roth, Coll. Works, Vol. 36   96 Piccadillies   edition hj. mayer, stuttgart, london

---

18
Covered print from '6 Piccadillies', 1969–70
Ironfilings on screenprinting on offsetprinting on card
on board under card under offsetprinting under
screenprinting
50 x 70 cm

Dieter Roth, Coll. Works, Vol. 36   96 Piccadillies   edition hj. mayer, stuttgart, london

19

Misprint from '6 Piccadillies', 1969–70
Screenprinting on offsetprinting on card on board under
card under offsetprinting under screenprinting
50 x 70 cm

Dieter Roth, Coll. Works, Vol. 36   96 Piccadillies   edition hj. mayer, stuttgart, london

---

20

Misprint from '6 Piccadillies', 1969–70
Screenprinting on offsetprinting on card on board under
card under offsetprinting under screenprinting
50 x 70 cm

Dieter Roth, Coll. Works, Vol. 36   96 Piccadillies   edition hj. mayer, stuttgart, london

21
Misprint from '6 Piccadillies', 1969–70
Screenprinting on offsetprinting on card on board under
card under offsetprinting under screenprinting
50 x 70 cm

Dieter Roth, Coll. Works, Vol. 36   96 Piccadillies   edition hj. mayer, stuttgart, london

22
Trial print from '6 Piccadillies', 1969–70
Screenprinting on offsetprinting on card on board under
card under offsetprinting under screenprinting
50 x 70 cm

Dieter Roth, Coll. Works, Vol. 36   96 Piccadillies   edition hj. mayer, stuttgart, london

23
Base-board from '6 Piccadillies', 1969–70
Screenprinting ink on screenprinting on offsetprinting
on card on board under card under offsetprinting under
screenprinting
50 x 70 cm

Dieter Roth, Coll. Works, Vol. 36   96 Piccadillies   edition hj. mayer, stuttgart, london

24
Trial print (back) from '6 Piccadillies', 1969–70
Screenprinting on offsetprinting on card on board under
card under offsetprinting under screenprinting
50 x 70 cm

Dieter Roth, Coll. Works, Vol. 36   96 Piccadillies   edition hj. mayer, stuttgart, london

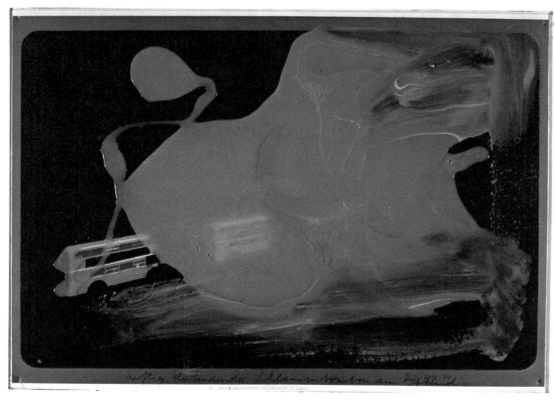

25
Grünsein wien Grünschwein, 1974
(Grünseier wien frürschwejh)
Glue and acrylic paint on screenprinting on
offsetprinting on card on board
50 x 70 cm

Dieter Roth, Coll. Works, Vol. 36   96 Piccadillies   edition hj. mayer, stuttgart, london

26
heftig blutendes Schlammbonbon am Abend, 1974
(heftiej ben Aindendis Schlammbonbon am abend)
Glue and acrylic paint on ironfilings on screenprinting
on offsetprinting on card on board
50 x 70 cm

Dieter Roth, Coll. Works, Vol. 36   96 Piccadillies   edition hj. mayer, stuttgart, london

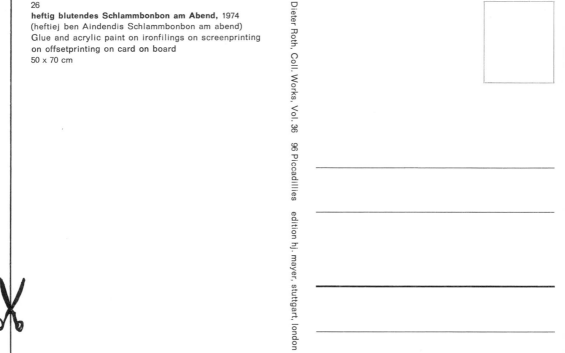

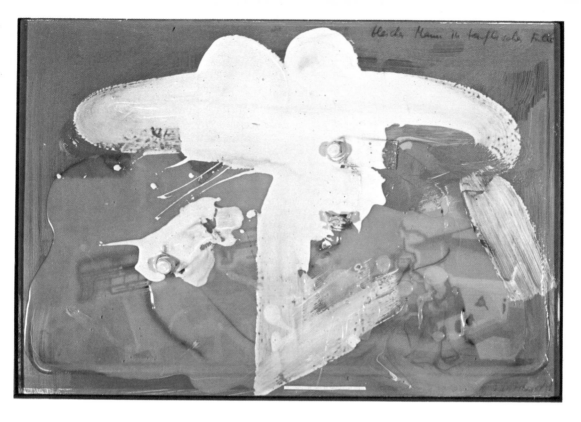

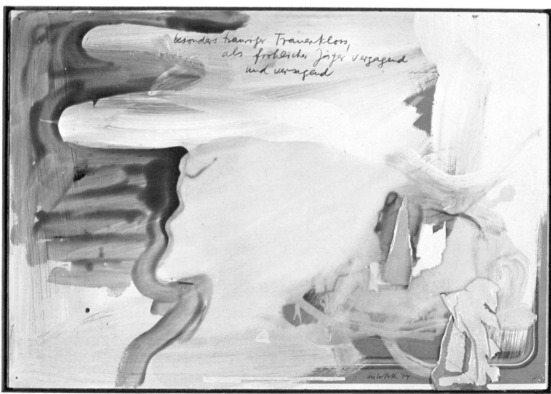

27
bleicher Mann in teuflischer Falle, 1974
(bleicher Mann in teuflischer Falle)
Acrylic paint and glue on screenprinting on
offsetprinting on card on board
50 x 70 cm

Dieter Roth, Coll. Works, Vol. 36   96 Piccadillies   edition hj. mayer, stuttgart, london

28
**besonders trauriger Trauerkloss, als fröhlicher Jäger
verzagend und versagend,** 1974
(besonders trauriger Trauerkloss, als frööklicher Jörger
vergagend und versagend)
Glue and acrylic paint on screenprinting on
offsetprinting on card on board
50 x 70 cm

Dieter Roth, Coll. Works, Vol. 36   96 Piccadillies   edition hj. mayer, stuttgart, london

mit Vogel Kacke sich ernährende fleische Schleimbonbonschmeissen   Dieter Roth 74

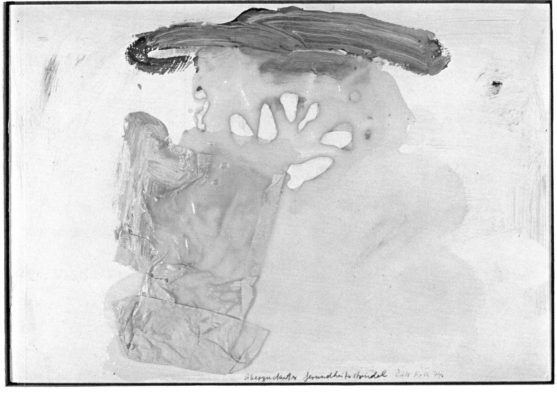

übergezuckerte Gesundheitsstrudel   Dieter Roth 74

29
**mit Vogelkacke sich ernährender, bleicher
Schleimbonbonschmeisser,** 1974
(mit Vogel karke sich ernahrender, bleicher
Schleimbonbon schmeissen)
Glue and acrylic paint on screenprinting on
offsetprinting on card on board
50 x 70 cm

Dieter Roth, Coll. Works, Vol. 36   96 Piccadillies   edition hj. mayer, stuttgart, london

30
überzuckerter Gesundheitsstrudel, 1974
(überzuckerts gesnudheits strudel)
Glue and acrylic paint on screenprinting on
offsetprinting on card on board
50 x 70 cm

Dieter Roth, Coll. Works, Vol. 36   96 Piccadillies   edition hj. mayer, stuttgart, london

4 Rübens Aftpumper an der Quelle

3 Engel

31

4 Rübensaftpumper an der Quelle, 1974
(4 Risbenseifspumper an der Quelle)
Glue and acrylic paint on screenprinting on
offsetprinting on card on board
50 x 70 cm

Dieter Roth, Coll. Works, Vol. 36   96 Piccadillies   edition hj. mayer, stuttgart, london

32

3 Engel als Zuckerpumper verkleidet, 1974
(3 Engel als zuckerpumps verkleidet)
Glue and acrylic paint on screenprinting on
offsetprinting on card on board
50 x 70 cm

Dieter Roth, Coll. Works, Vol. 36   96 Piccadillies   edition hj. mayer, stuttgart, london

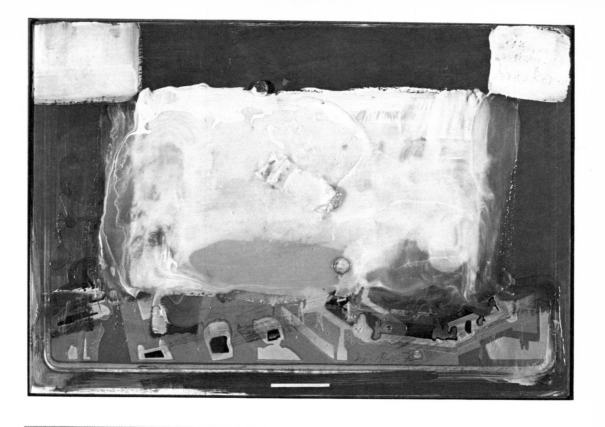

33
ein bleicher Kracker, 1974
(ein bleicher Kracker)
Acrylic paint and glue on screenprinting on
offsetprinting on card on board
50 x 70 cm

Dieter Roth, Coll. Works, Vol. 36   96 Piccadillies   edition hj. mayer, stuttgart, london

34
**2 Schwätzer, am Abend als stille Nachtwächter
auftretend,** 1974
(2 Schwätger, am Abend als stille Nachtwächter
auftretend)
Glue and acrylic paint on screenprinting on
offsetprinting on card on board
50 x 70 cm

Dieter Roth, Coll. Works, Vol. 36   96 Piccadillies   edition hj. mayer, stuttgart, london

deutscher Teufel,
als getarnte
Schokoladenbombe
versagend

2 Kartoffelknödel

35
**deutscher Teufel, als gekreuzigte Schokoladenbombe
versagend,** 1974
(denfaher Teufel, als getsenjigle Schokoladenbombe
versgend)
Glue and acrylic paint on ironfilings on screenprinting
on offsetprinting on card on board
50 x 70 cm

Dieter Roth, Coll. Works, Vol. 36   96 Piccadillies   edition hj. mayer, stuttgart, london

36
2 Kartobbelknaben, 1974
Glue and acrylic paint on screenprinting on
offsetprinting on card on board
50 x 70 cm

Dieter Roth, Coll. Works, Vol. 36   96 Piccadillies   edition hj. mayer, stuttgart, london

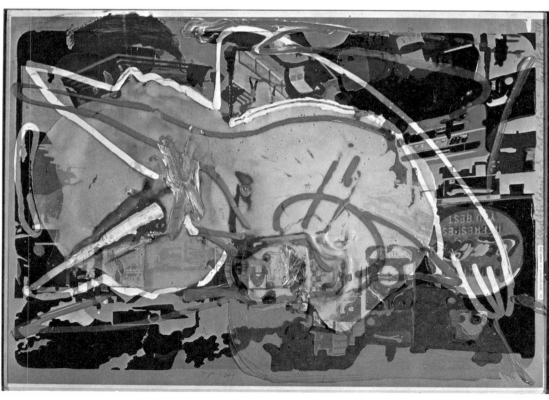

37
Trauer ohne Hende, 1974
(Trans ohne Hende)
Glue and acrylic paint on screenprinting on
offsetprinting on card on board
50 x 70 cm

Dieter Roth, Coll. Works, Vol. 36   96 Piccadillies   edition hj. mayer, stuttgart, london

38
Selbstbildnis als Pulverfass, 1974
(Self-portrait as powder keg)
Acrylic paint and glue on screenprinting on
offsetprinting on card on board
70 x 50 cm

Dieter Roth, Coll. Works, Vol. 36   96 Piccadillies   edition hj. mayer, stuttgart, london

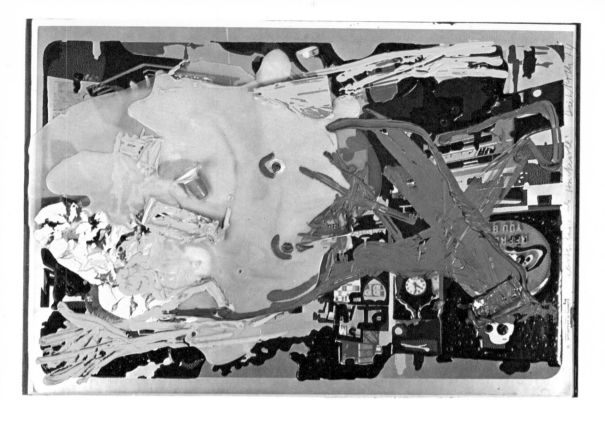

39
Selbstbildnis als Huckevoll, 1974
(Self-portrait as hucke voll)
Acrylic paint, glue and collage on screenprinting
on offsetprinting on card on board
70 x 50 cm

Dieter Roth, Coll. Works, Vol. 36 96 Piccadillies edition hj. mayer, stuttgart, london

40
Selbstbildnis als Kraft zur Tat, 1974
(Self-portrait as kraft zur tat)
Acrylic paint and glue on screenprinting on
offsetprinting on card on board
50 x 70 cm

Dieter Roth, Coll. Works, Vol. 36 96 Piccadillies edition hj. mayer, stuttgart, london

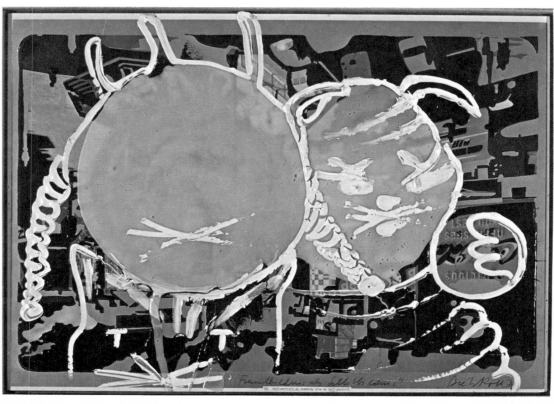

41
Selbstbild als Telefondraht, 1974
(Self-portrait as telephone wire)
Acrylic paint and glue on screenprinting on
offsetprinting on card on board
50 x 70 cm

Dieter Roth, Coll. Works, Vol. 36   96 Piccadillies   edition hj. mayer, stuttgart, london

42
Fremdbildnis als Selbstbildnis, 1974
(Self-portrait as somebody else as self-portrait)
Acrylic paint and glue on screenprinting on
offsetprinting on card on board
50 x 70 cm

Dieter Roth, Coll. Works, Vol. 36   96 Piccadillies   edition hj. mayer, stuttgart, london

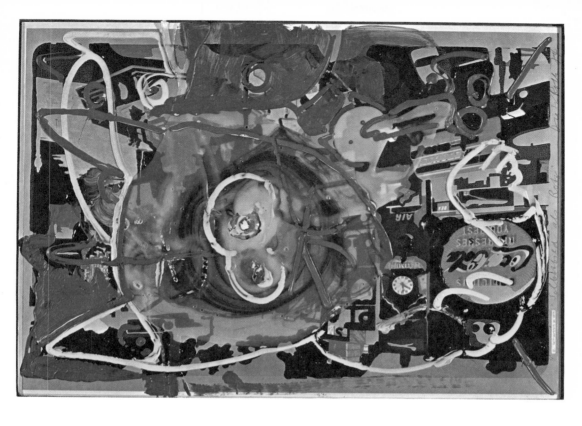

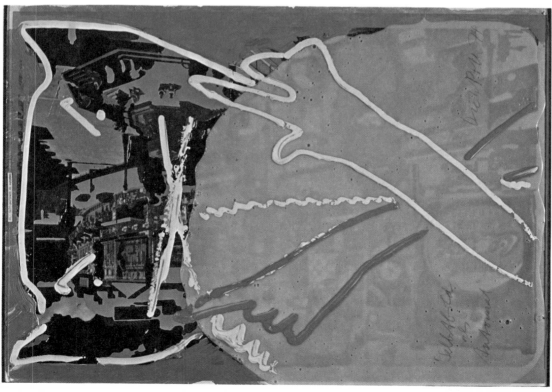

Dieter Roth, Coll. Works, Vol. 36   96 Piccadillies   edition hj. mayer, stuttgart, london

43
Selbstbild als Rotz, 1974
(Self-portrait as shit)
Acrylic paint and glue on screenprinting on
offsetprinting on card on board
70 x 50 cm

Dieter Roth, Coll. Works, Vol. 36   96 Piccadillies   edition hj. mayer, stuttgart, london

44
Selbstbild als Automat, 1974
(Self-portrait as Automat)
Glue and acrylic paint on screenprinting on
offsetprinting on card on board
70 x 50 cm

"Selbstbildnis als Hausfrau"

30. Self-portrait as another housewife

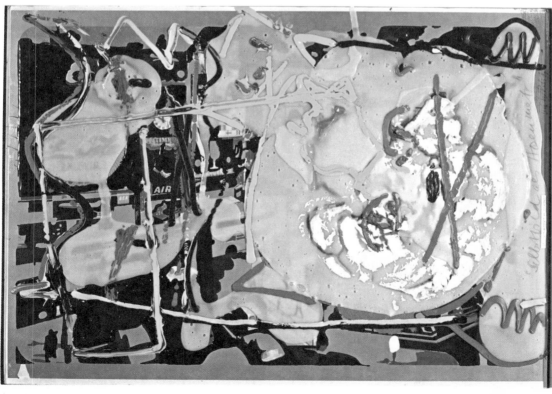

45
Selbstbildnis als andere Hausfrau, 1974
(Self-portrait as another housewife)
Acrylic paint, glue and collage on screenprinting
on offsetprinting on card on board
50 x 70 cm

Dieter Roth, Coll. Works, Vol. 36   96 Piccadillies   edition hj. mayer, stuttgart, london

46
Selbstbild als Hosenmatz, 1974
(Self-portrait as hosenmatz)
Glue, acrylic paint and collage on screenprinting
on offsetprinting on card on board
70 x 50 cm

Dieter Roth, Coll. Works, Vol. 36   96 Piccadillies   edition hj. mayer, stuttgart, london

47
Selbstbild als Kackindieluft, 1974
(Self-portrait as shitintheair)
Acrylic paint on screenprinting on offsetprinting
on card on board
50 x 70 cm

Dieter Roth, Coll. Works, Vol. 36   96 Piccadillies   edition hj. mayer, stuttgart, london

48
Selbstbildnis an der Wand, 1974
(Self-portrtait as wall)
Acrylic paint and glue on screenprinting on
offsetprinting on card on board
50 x 70 cm

Dieter Roth, Coll. Works, Vol. 36   96 Piccadillies   edition hj. mayer, stuttgart, london

Freundbildnis unter Bekannte   Dieter Roth 74

83. Portrait of someone else among acquaintances

49
Fremdbildnis unter Bekannten, 1974
(Portrait of someone else among acquaintances)
Acrylic paint and glue on screenprinting on
offsetprinting on card on board
50 x 70 cm

Dieter Roth, Coll. Works, Vol. 36   96 Piccadillies   edition hj. mayer, stuttgart, london

50
Selbstbild unter Fremden, 1974
(Portrait of someone else among foreigners)
Glue and acrylic paint on screenprinting on
offsetprinting on card on board
70 x 50 cm

Dieter Roth, Coll. Works, Vol. 36   96 Piccadillies   edition hj. mayer, stuttgart, london

Selbstbild als Euerbach

Dieter Roth 74

82. Self-portrait as Feuerbach

Selbstbild — als Selbst-portrait

Dieter Roth 74

83. Project of a self-portrait

51

Selbstbild als Eisenbart, 1974
(Self-portrait as iron beard)
Glue and acrylic paint on screenprinting on
offsetprinting on card on board
50 x 70 cm

Dieter Roth, Coll. Works, Vol. 36 96 Piccadillies edition hj. mayer, stuttgart, london

52

Selbstbildnis als Selbstportrait, 1974
(Picture of a self-portrait)
Acrylic paint and glue on screenprinting on
offsetprinting on card on board
70 x 50 cm

Dieter Roth, Coll. Works, Vol. 36 96 Piccadillies edition hj. mayer, stuttgart, london

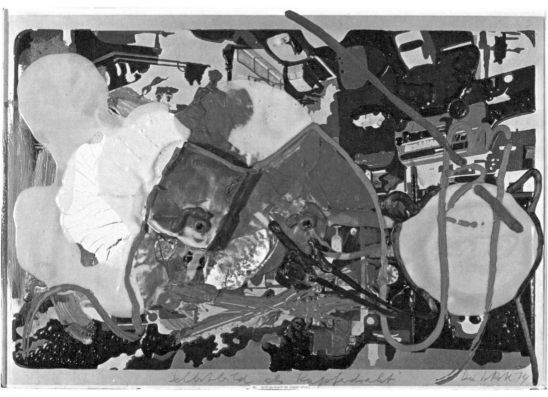

53
Selbstbild als Hasenschaukel, 1974
(Self-portrait as hasen schaukel)
Acrylic paint, glue and collage on screenprinting
on offsetprinting on card on board
70 x 50 cm

Dieter Roth, Coll. Works, Vol. 36   96 Piccadillies   edition hj. mayer, stuttgart, london

54
Selbstbild als Kupferdraht, 1974
(Self-portrait as copper wire)
Glue and acrylic paint on screenprinting on
offsetprinting on card on board
50 x 70 cm

Dieter Roth, Coll. Works, Vol. 36   96 Piccadillies   edition hj. mayer, stuttgart, london

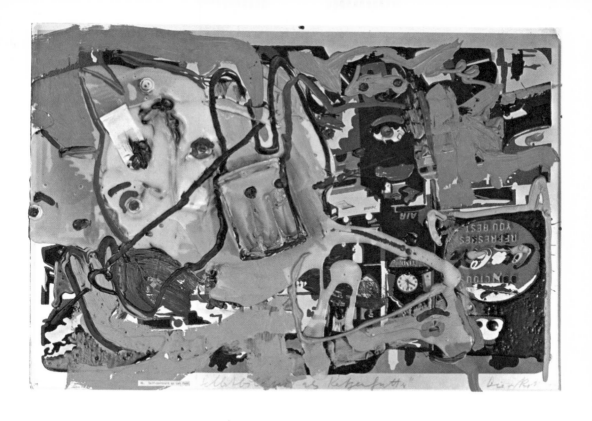

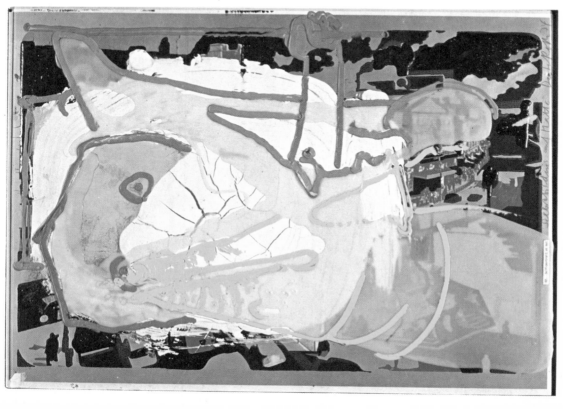

55

Selbstbildnis als Katzenfutter, 1974
(Self-portrait as cat food)
Acrylic paint, glue and collage on screenprinting
on offsetprinting on card on board
50 x 70 cm

Dieter Roth, Coll. Works, Vol. 36   96 Piccadillies   edition hj. mayer, stuttgart, london

56

Selbstbildnis auf Matte, 1974
(Self-portrait on mat)
Glue and acrylic paint on screenprinting on
offsetprinting on card on board
70 x 50 cm

Dieter Roth, Coll. Works, Vol. 36   96 Piccadillies   edition hj. mayer, stuttgart, london

Selbstbild als Herkules — Self-portrait as Hercules — Dieter Roth 74

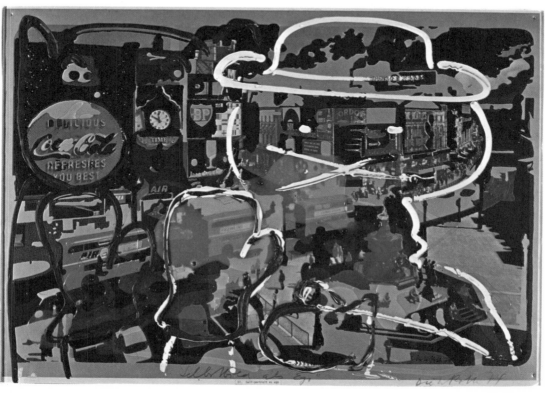

Selbstbild als Ego — Self-portrait as ego — Dieter Roth 74

57
Selbstbildnis als Herkules, 1974
(Self-portrait as Hercules)
Glue and acrylic paint on screenprinting on
offsetprinting on card on board
50 x 70 cm

Dieter Roth, Coll. Works, Vol. 36   96 Piccadillies   edition hj. mayer, stuttgart, london

58
Selbstbild als Ego, 1974
(Self-portrait as ego)
Acrylic paint and glue on screenprinting on
offsetprinting on card on board
50 x 70 cm

Dieter Roth, Coll. Works, Vol. 36   96 Piccadillies   edition hj. mayer, stuttgart, london

"Selbstbild als Sau" Uwe L Rösch 74

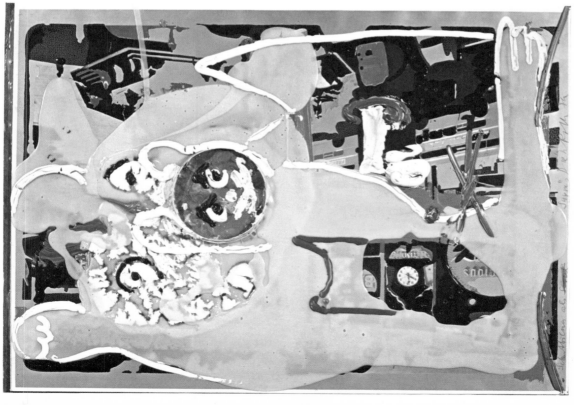

59

Selbstbild als Sau, 1974
(Self-portrait as sow)
Acrylic paint on screenprinting on offsetprinting
on card on board
50 x 70 cm

Dieter Roth, Coll. Works, Vol. 36   96 Piccadillies   edition hj. mayer, stuttgart, london

60

Selbstbildnis als Suppe, 1974
(Self-pictured soup)
Glue, acrylic paint and collage on screenprinting
on offsetprinting on card on board
70 x 50 cm

Dieter Roth, Coll. Works, Vol. 36   96 Piccadillies   edition hj. mayer, stuttgart, london

Red, Brown and Green Buses waving Banners at E.O.

Surprisingly empty stage, surprisingly crowded

61

Red Person and Green Being waving Banners at E.O.,
1976
Ink and acrylic paint on offsetprinting on card on board
on hardboard
39 x 55 cm

Dieter Roth, Coll. Works, Vol. 36   96 Piccadillies   edition hj. mayer, stuttgart, london

62

Surprisingly empty stage, surprisingly crowded, 1976
Acrylic paint and glue on offsetprinting on card
on board an hardboard
39 x 55 cm

Dieter Roth, Coll. Works, Vol. 36   96 Piccadillies   edition hj. mayer, stuttgart, london

Flakes Out of The Grey

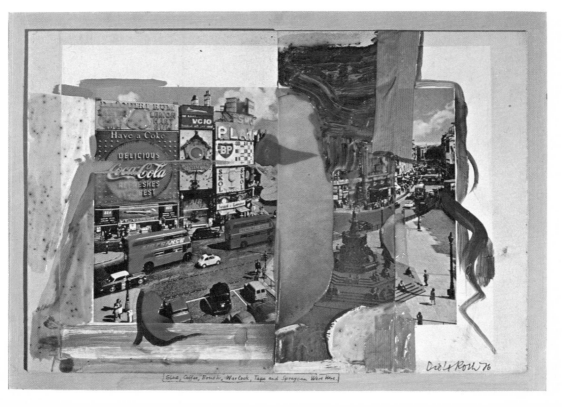

Glue, Coffee, Brush, Warlock, Tape and Spraycan Were Here.

63
Flakes Out of The Grey, 1976
Pencil, ink and acrylic paint on offsetprinting
on card on board on hardboard
39 x 55 cm

Dieter Roth, Coll. Works, Vol. 36   96 Piccadillies   edition hj. mayer, stuttgart, london

64
**Glue, Coffee, Brush, Warlock, Tape and Spraycan
Where Here.,** 1976
Glue, acrylic paint, coffee grindings and collage on
offsetprinting on card on board on hardboard
39 x 55 cm

Dieter Roth, Coll. Works, Vol. 36   96 Piccadillies   edition hj. mayer, stuttgart, london

"Look at that Sad Place where Lollipop exploded has! >> - << Silo, I cannot see said Place, Lollipop has blown out my Memory! !!"

Dieter Roth 72

Piece of a Printed Scene (Unpainted)

Dieter Roth 72

65
**«Look at that Sad Place where Lollipop explodes has!» –
«No, I cannot see said Place, Lollipop has blown out
my Memory!»,** 1976
Acrylic paint and collage on offsetprinting on card
on board on hardboard
39 x 55 cm

Dieter Roth, Coll. Works, Vol. 36   96 Piccadillies   edition hj. mayer, stuttgart, london

66
Peace of a Printed Scene (unpainted), 1976
Offsetprinting on card on cardboard on hardboard
39 x 55 cm

Dieter Roth, Coll. Works, Vol. 36   96 Piccadillies   edition hj. mayer, stuttgart, london

Buster's Plain Melody, played on a Busted Canopy - Where is it ?

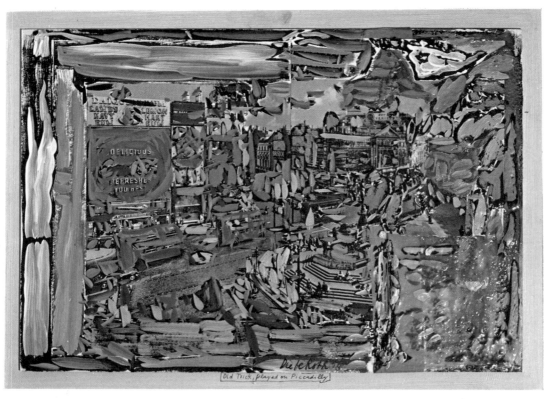

Old Trick, played on Piccadilly

67

**Buster's Plain Melody played on a Busted Canopy –
Were is It?,** 1976
Acrylic paint and collage on offsetprinting on card
on board on hardboard
39 x 55 cm

Dieter Roth, Coll. Works, Vol. 36   96 Piccadillies   edition hj. mayer, stuttgart, london

68

Old Trick, Played on Piccadilly, 1976
Acrylic paint, glue and collage on offsetprinting on card
on board on hardboard
39 x 55 cm

Dieter Roth, Coll. Works, Vol. 36   96 Piccadillies   edition hj. mayer, stuttgart, london

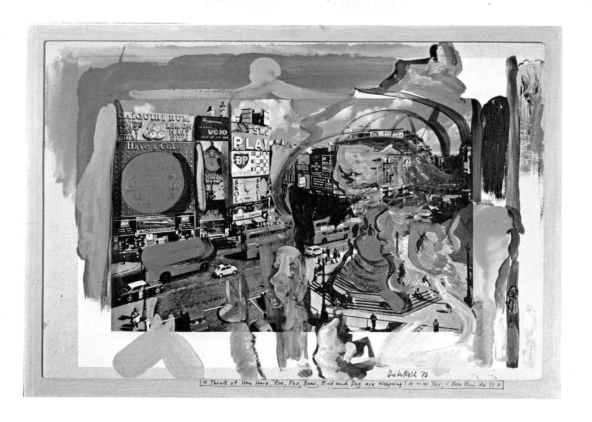

«Think of How Hare, Roe, Fox, Bear, Bird and Dog are weeping!» — «Yes, I Hear How do It.»

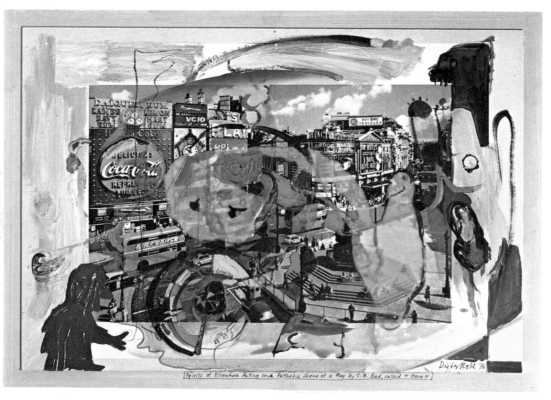

Spirits of Elsewhere Acting in a Pathetic Scene at a Play by C.B. Sad, called «Here»

69

**"Think of How Hare, Roe, Fox, Bear, Bird and Dog
are weeping!" – "Yes, I Hear them do It.",** 1976
Acrylic paint and glue on offsetprinting on card
on board on hardboard
39 x 55 cm

Dieter Roth, Coll. Works, Vol. 36   96 Piccadillies   edition hj. mayer, stuttgart, london

70

**Spirits of Elsewhere Acting in Pathetic Scene of
a Play by C. S. Sad, called "Here",** 1976
Pencil, acrylic paint, glue and collage on offsetprinting
on card on board on hardboard
39 x 55 cm

Dieter Roth, Coll. Works, Vol. 36   96 Piccadillies   edition hj. mayer, stuttgart, london

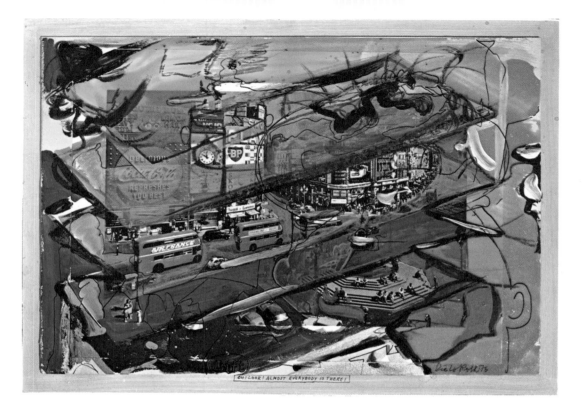

OH! LOOK! ALMOST EVERYBODY IS THERE!

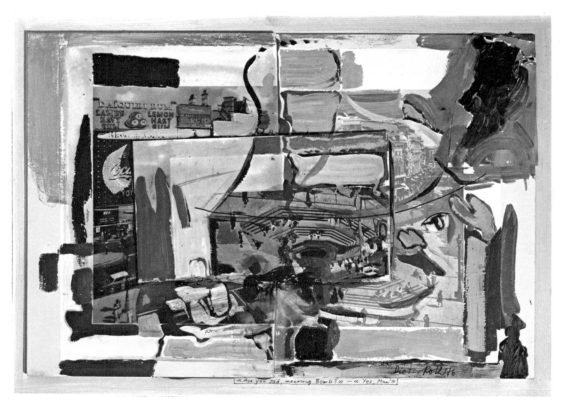

«Are you sad, meaning Bomb?» — «Yes, Man!»

71

OH! LOOK! ALMOST EVERYBODY IS THERE!, 1976
Ink, crayon and acrylic paint on offsetprinting on card
on board on hardboard
39 x 55 cm

Dieter Roth, Coll. Works, Vol. 36   96 Piccadillies   edition hj. mayer, stuttgart, london

72

"Are you sad, menacing Bomb?" – "Yes, Man!", 1976
Pencil, ink, acrylic paint and collage on offsetprinting
on card on board on hardboard
39 x 55 cm

Dieter Roth, Coll. Works, Vol. 36   96 Piccadillies   edition hj. mayer, stuttgart, london

Cut Up Narcissus, Crumbling

Rabbits Dancing on Hay under the Clouds

73
Cut Up Narcissus, Crumbling, 1976
Acrylic paint, glue and collage on offsetprinting
on card on board on hardboard
39 x 55 cm

Dieter Roth, Coll. Works, Vol. 36   96 Piccadillies   edition hj. mayer, stuttgart, london

74
Rabbits Dancing on Hay under the Clouds, 1976
Ink, glue, acrylic paint, chocolate and collage
on offsetprinting on card on board on hardboard
39 x 55 cm

Dieter Roth, Coll. Works, Vol. 36   96 Piccadillies   edition hj. mayer, stuttgart, london

Gardener's Nerves
Looking into Palm trees?

David Roth 76

David Roth 76

« Who Painting is Good Orange and Blue Pictures, These Days? » « Fucking Jackson It Is! »

75
"Gardener's Nerves, Looking like Palmtrees", 1976
Pencil, oil-pastels, acrylic paint and collage
on offsetprinting on card on board on hardboard
39 x 55 cm

Dieter Roth, Coll. Works, Vol. 36   96 Piccadillies   edition hj. mayer, stuttgart, london

76
**"Who Painting Is Good Orange and Blue Pictures,
These Days?" "Fucking Sucker It Is!",** 1976
Acrylic paint on offsetprinting on card on board
on hardboard
39 x 55 cm

Dieter Roth, Coll. Works, Vol. 36   96 Piccadillies   edition hj. mayer, stuttgart, london

"7 Egos' Compound's Review" Dieter Roth 76

Triple-Breasted Melody was Here Dieter Roth 76

77
"7 Egos' Compound's Preview", 1976
Acrylic paint on offsetprinting on card on cardboard
on hardboard
39 x 55 cm

Dieter Roth, Coll. Works, Vol. 36   96 Piccadillies   edition hj. mayer, stuttgart, london

78
Triple-Breasted Melody was Here, 1976
Oil-pastels and acrylic paint on offsetprinting on card
on cardboard on hardboard
39 x 55 cm

Dieter Roth, Coll. Works, Vol. 36   96 Piccadillies   edition hj. mayer, stuttgart, london

A Look Into The Hares' Nest

Winter of the DOGS & HUNTERS

79
A Look Into The Hares' Nest, 1976
Pencil, ink, glue, acrylic paint and oil-pastels
on offsetprinting on card on cardboard on hardboard
39 x 55 cm

Dieter Roth, Coll. Works, Vol. 36   96 Piccadillies   edition hj. mayer, stuttgart, london

80
Winter at the DOGS & HUNTERS, 1976
Pencil, ink, oil-pastels, glue and acrylic paint
on offsetprinting on card on board on hardboard
39 x 55 cm

Dieter Roth, Coll. Works, Vol. 36   96 Piccadillies   edition hj. mayer, stuttgart, london

«Look! They Are Devouring Each Other!» - © D.Roth ©

Game 3   After the Play or before the Play   Dieter Roth 76

81
"Look! They Are Devouring Each Other!" – "O.K.!", 1976
Pencil, ink, glue, acrylic paint and oil-pastels
on offsetprinting on card on cardboard on hardboard
39 x 55 cm

Dieter Roth, Coll. Works, Vol. 36   96 Piccadillies   edition hj. mayer, stuttgart, london

82
Games After the Play or Before the Play, 1976
Acrylic paint and glue on offsetprinting on card
on board on hardboard
39 x 55 cm

Dieter Roth, Coll. Works, Vol. 36   96 Piccadillies   edition hj. mayer, stuttgart, london

Blue Window Singing Orange Song

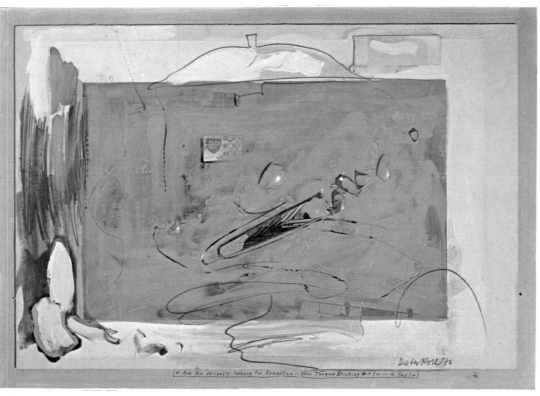

Are you seriously looking for Ernestine – Your Tongue Sticking Out too – « Yes! »

83
Blue Window Singing Orange Song, 1976
Acrylic paint, glue and chocolate on offsetprinting
on card on board on hardboard
39 x 55 cm

Dieter Roth, Coll. Works, Vol. 36   96 Piccadillies   edition hj. mayer, stuttgart, london

84
**"Are You seriously looking for Ernestine – Your Tongue
Sticking Out?" – "Yes!",** 1976
Pencil, ink, acrylic paint, glue and collage
on offsetprinting on card on board on hardboard
39 x 55 cm

Dieter Roth, Coll. Works, Vol. 36   96 Piccadillies   edition hj. mayer, stuttgart, london

« This is what you see when you look out of this window. » — « Oh, I see! »

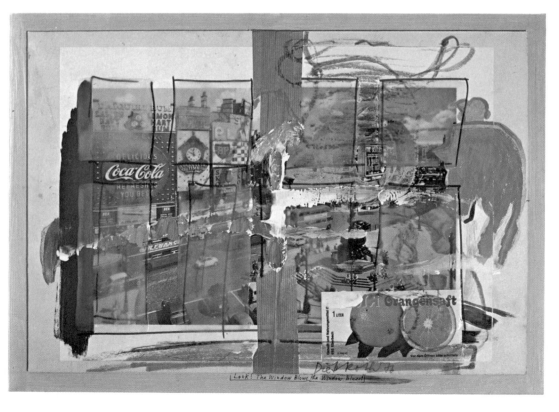

Look! The Window Blows the Window Blues!

85
**"This is what you see when you look out of
this window." – "Oh, I see!"**, 1976
Pencil, acrylic paint and collage on offsetprinting
on card on board on hardboard
39 x 55 cm

Dieter Roth, Coll. Works, Vol. 36   96 Piccadillies   edition hj. mayer, stuttgart, london

86
Look! The Window Blows the Window Blues!, 1976
Acrylic paint, glue, oil-pastels and collage
on offsetprinting on card on board on hardboard
39 x 55 cm

Dieter Roth, Coll. Works, Vol. 36   96 Piccadillies   edition hj. mayer, stuttgart, london

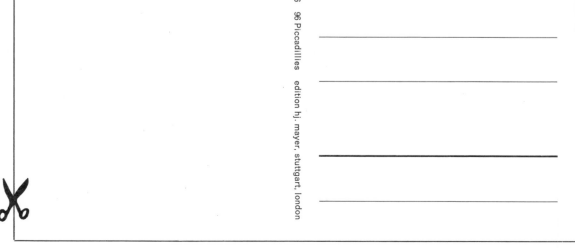

[Hare and Man Trapped on Stage complaining]

[" Yes, I do fear You ! "]

87
Hare and Man Trapped on Stage, Complaining, 1976
Pencil, ink, acrylic paint and glue on offsetprinting
on card on board on hardboard
39 x 55 cm

Dieter Roth, Coll. Works, Vol. 36   96 Piccadillies   edition hj. mayer, stuttgart, london

88
"Yes, I Do fear You!", 1976
Acrylic paint and glue on offsetprinting on card
on board on hardboard
39 x 55 cm

Dieter Roth, Coll. Works, Vol. 36   96 Piccadillies   edition hj. mayer, stuttgart, london

Ah, There, Yellow And Hairy, Misplaced Tripalsuckas!!

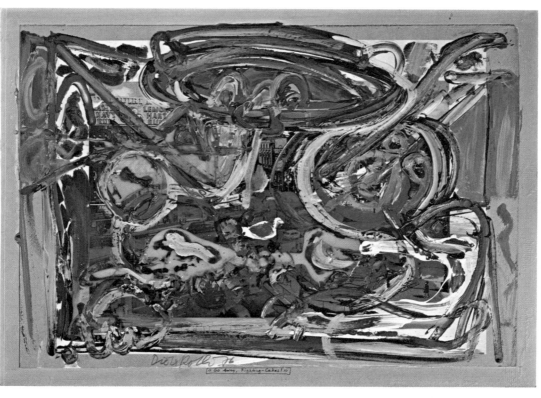

Go Away, Fighting-Cakes!!!

89
Ah, There, Yellow And Hairy, Misplaced Tripelsuckers!!,
1976
Acrylic paint, oil-pastels and collage on offsetprinting
on card on cardboard on hardboard
39 x 55 cm

Dieter Roth, Coll. Works, Vol. 36   96 Piccadillies   edition hj. mayer, stuttgart, london

90
"Go Away, Fighting-Cakes!", 1976
Acrylic paint and glue on offsetprinting on card
on cardboard on hardboard
39 x 55 cm

Dieter Roth, Coll. Works, Vol. 36   96 Piccadillies   edition hj. mayer, stuttgart, london

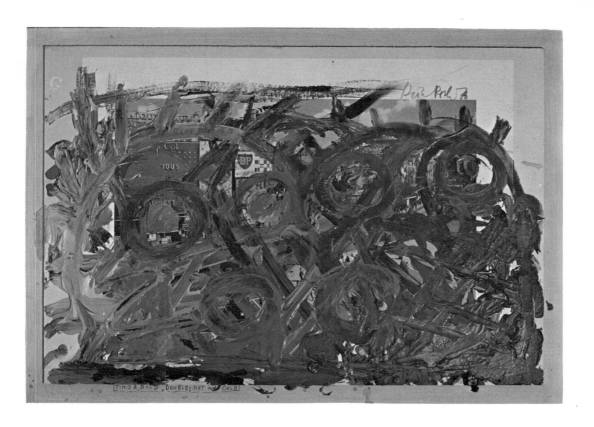

TIMID & BOLD - DOUBLE: HOT and COLD]

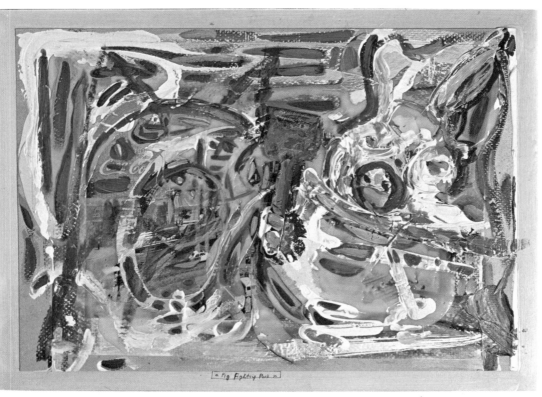

Pig Eighty Pork

91

TIMID & BOLD DOUBLE; HOT and COLD, 1976
Acrylic paint on offsetprinting on card on board
on hardboard
39 x 55 cm

Dieter Roth, Coll. Works, Vol. 36   96 Piccadillies   edition hj. mayer, stuttgart, london

92

"Pig Fighting Pork", 1976
Acrylic paint, glue and collage on offsetprinting
on card on cardboard on hardboard
39 x 55 cm

Dieter Roth, Coll. Works, Vol. 36   96 Piccadillies   edition hj. mayer, stuttgart, london

Sunset Transplanted

Scene, Cold and Bold

93
Sunset Transplanted, 1976
Ink, acrylic paint and collage on offsetprinting on card
on board on hardboard
39 x 55 cm

Dieter Roth, Coll. Works, Vol. 36   96 Piccadillies   edition hj. mayer, stuttgart, london

94
Scene, Cold and Bold, 1976
Acrylic paint on offsetprinting on card on cardboard
on hardboard
39 x 55 cm

Dieter Roth, Coll. Works, Vol. 36   96 Piccadillies   edition hj. mayer, stuttgart, london

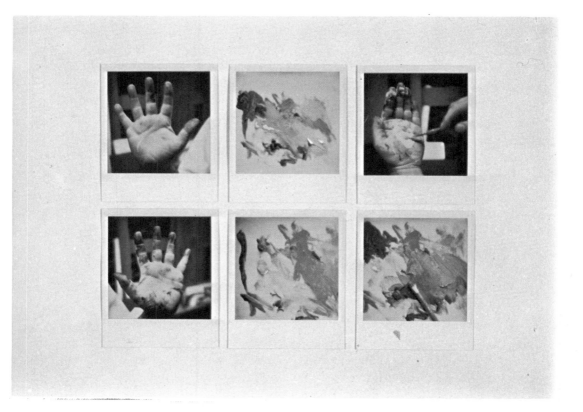

95
Piccadilly from 'COLLABORATIONS OF CH. ROTHAM',
1976/77
(with Richard Hamilton)
Acrylic paint and enamel on screenprinting on cloth
ca 50 x 75 cm

Dieter Roth, Coll. Works, Vol. 36   96 Piccadillies   edition hj. mayer, stuttgart, london

96
**Certificate for Piccadilly from 'COLLABORATIONS
OF CH. ROTHAM',** 1976/77
(with Richard Hamilton)
Acrylic paint and enamel on polaroids on paper
30 x 42 cm

Dieter Roth, Coll. Works, Vol. 36   96 Piccadillies   edition hj. mayer, stuttgart, london

DIETER ROTH
AN INTRODUCTION
by
Dieter Schwarz

"If I now look more precisely at my insignificant form, which sits near the doors in the literary parish room, I perceive it belongs to that dubious band of spirits which ploughs with two ploughs and in the reference books bears the name 'painter and poet'. They are the ones, in whose poems the Philistine at times approvingly applauds: Aha, here you see the painter! and before whose paintings: Here you see the poet! The more naïve among them indulge in such praise, but others who do not forget their Lessing, feel their life troubled by it and it irritates them whenever the matter is spoken of. Those comfortably continue to blow on the double flute, these deny themselves a reed at the first opportunity, so sorry they are."
Gottfried Keller, **Autobiography (1876)**

As far as a biography can help . . . Here we shall merely try to follow the name from **dieter roth** to **Dieter Roth,** another route may well lead to the personality, but we do not seek this, we remain entranced by the splendour of the pictures or are infatuated by their gloom, we must become bogged down between the pages of the books. The name is traversing all books and pictures since **dieter roth** published a wood cut for the first time in 1953 in the periodical **spirale,** which he had founded with Eugen Gomringer and Marcel Wyss and initially also edited. The name is written all ways and consequently leads one to think that the products of the author may be regarded or read as different ones, – that even the same text, printed in different editions, has differed from itself at least in terms of time, that at least a sense of distance has crept into the text, which does not allow it to remain the same. Now when **diter rot** signs in Iceland, where he has lived for the most part since 1957, it is not only the withdrawal to the island which has removed the name. When in contact with the Swiss art of the fifties, which is dominated by the concrete artists (Bill, Lohse, Graeser), he becomes aware of the formal reductions, the desire for clarity, simplicity, of the resolve to reject and throw away everything vague, superfluous, indistinct. The letters which are dropped from the name, do they allow form to follow function more closely? The fact that the name most strikingly grasps at purism because standing in focus is surely comment enough. Who could fail to follow? However, this excursion or may we rather say this incursion into orthography can be taken further: on the whole letters which occur in the double form in German are eliminated, the usual combinations to represent certain sounds are simplified, and letters which can only be explained by tradition are deleted; his own writing develops from the more or less consistent literal reforms which alienates the texts, makes them difficult to read, gives them a new visual shape and which finally leads the regularity of the logically arranged visual forms of concrete art to falter in another field. Falter, if one remembers the intentions behind them. The optical result which his texts evoke and which cannot be explained on the basis of functional criteria is a first effort to place different things side by side without forming superior concepts, a model showing that every representation is arbitrary even if it seeks to resort to predetermined certainty and validity, and that it is primarily dependent upon its own laws as far as readability is concerned. Yet at the same time he always works within language (particularly the German language), and so avoids making arbitrariness completely his own, a mistake which opens the way to artistic privacy of insignificance. Even if the new conception of writing only lasts to the early sixties, **diter rot** will remain, and after one or two starts of **DITER ROT** will not rely on **dieter rot** until the **collected works** are to appear. With the increasing output of books the name is being tossed to and fro, regains its old **dieter roth** and finally puts an end to the uninterrupted small writing which still derives from the concept of civilization's progress of the fifties, as it resumes the practice of capitalization (which is crossing the German language on winding roads) – one possibility of differentiation which **Dieter Roth** cannot deny himself. With the ramification of the shit books, which are a challenge to variety, the name is enlarged to **Dieterich Roth** and to **Karl-Dietrich Roth**, making use of the full Christian name, the distant, the all embracing. Perhaps these references already may show that the irritating method of writing, which perplexed many critics, was not just a joke but a precise unfolding of the problems which are posed when the author signs his works, knots of lines which have not been untied by this, but continue to become more and more involved in themselves.

The artist, called in the following **D. R.**, not only moved within the scope of his own work, however, which could at last be described and classified as a result of stylistic developments. His encounter with other artists is so important to him since he is not afraid to borrow, to try out styles, but always endeavouring to reverse what has been borrowed into its opposite and to mark the styles as recognisable, laughable and interchangeable. He gets into close co-operation with Stefan Wewerka in 1970 (but some series of works have been made before): they set about doing drawings in which they choose the most trivial motifs and cheapest sketchy means in order to tell frivolous, pictorial jokes. The collision, or better the often gentle discharging of the lines is intended to make the point of the respective failure all the clearer, this crash which can at most cause a chuckle. Beside this there are multi-layered graphics in which the pictorial invention of the one is taken further by the other, so that the ambiguity already present is increased in the turning of both attack and direction.

From the many years of friendship with Richard Hamilton a few joint graphics emanated in the sixties, until in the summer of 1976 a new kind of picture is invented in Spain with the **Collaborations of Ch. Rotham.** Pictures which in some cases have already been carefully prepared by Hamilton are quickly retouched by D. R. so that by the use of extremely exaggerated, impossible formations a pictorial plan is carried away into areas which must be frightening both working artists and observers, and which profit by the fear of the daub, the embittered and the sweetened. With each picture is supplied a

certificate which once again represents the "preliminary picture", as skil-
fully as possible, and also as seductively so that the observer becomes
reconciled to it. What is here shown as respect is only yet another blow
which comes even harder since it is suffered so readily. Together with
Hamilton (English) texts have been written too which make use of the pictures and their means of production only as an occasion to cope with one
another once again, and in which the covering and overrolling writing of D. R.
does not play off the chaos against the elaborated style but endeavours to
wipe out his tracks in the writing itself, in order to signify them. The double
game of original and certificate is taken over by the new series of pictures
they did in 1977, the **INTERFACEs,** thirty pairs of double self portraits which
relate the pictorial splitting up with the disintegrating effects of intersubjec-
tivity.

Perhaps the most continuous co-operation can be seen in the founding of the
firm **Rainer & Roth,** which has been in business since 1973, and which was
given the trade mark **Mix- u. Trennkunst** (Mix and Separate Art). Arnulf
Rainer had previously only worked for himself and had unassailably built up
his superpaintings and poses. His contribution to the co-operation lies essen-
tially in his stubborn resistance, his constant readiness to isolate himself, and
even to expose D. R. or to cover him by this. Thus his often humble manner,
which he shows, for example, in photoseries or in video work, is also a trap
which merely forces the stronger person to adapt himself to the weaker person on whom he must still rely. It is also striking in these works that a clear
distinction is often made between the respective contributions, so that
attempts are made to have an equal picture executed by the two side by side,
which emphasise even more strongly the peculiarities, the slight slipping off
into mannerism of the painters, both of them deciding then to treat their
inability seriously, to promote it still further, to drive it forward and to act it
out dramatically. No longer to be afraid of stale jokes, idiotic strokes and
huge financial claims addressed to the public, requires the great courage in
detaching from pretensions which are so easily raised when considering
pictures. The firm which appears here is a new name under which it is
allowed to engage in activities such as the printing of business forms which
translate the decided nothing into the language of the market.

In addition there is the one-week literary joint production of the **1. Berliner
Dichter-Workshop** (1st Poetry Workshop Berlin), which besides D. R. brought
together Friedrich Achleitner, Günter Brus, Gerhard Rühm and Oswald Wiener. From this was also formed the concept of joint musical performances,
the **selten gehörte musik** (rarely heard music). Some concerts were given in
Munich, Berlin, Hamburg and Karlsruhe together with Brus, Rühm, Wiener
and Hermann Nitsch, advances towards an ultimate music, a clearance sale
of styles, starts towards pathos, miniature episodes surrendering to their own
melancholy, the overblowing and striking out of what is quietly remembered
and dawning in the head.

As D. R. played solo a **Quadrupelkonzert** (quadruple concert) in Basle 1977, in which the performance is finally lost in the roaring of the multiple layers of playback sound material and in the constant cancellation of the performance, it is not so easy to put him down merely as a painter-poet. At least a triple, at least a painter-poet-musician who plays quartets with himself. The quartets of the unfolding of what is to be represented, which cannot be played off, since in the end the determination of what has been gained is not at stake, as it wanders game after game from hand to hand. Thus the question is not raised anymore as to whether this or that is the true profession, – the hovering over all positions is disturbing not for the vacant decision but for the constant dwelling on detours which make vanish the final destination falsely attributed by the inquirers. Even if the books represent the point to which all his work is directed this does not mean that he so easily renounces the other possibilities. The books are so important because in them everything is possible, because one book may also contain hundreds of pictures and even a few symphonies. The paintings, graphics, records, everything else which could be attached to make an organ out of the double flute, is written down in the books and fills page for page easily and colourfully.

II

"The brown vine slopes reflect beautifully in the water, the country houses too. Of course! One and the other must be reflected. None has any preference. Everything which enlivens the bank in form and colour is subject to the lake, which does with it what it wants to do. It reflects it. It is the magician, the master, the fairy-tale, the picture."
Robert Walser, **Fritz Kocher's Compositions**

D. R.'s work on books can seldom be equated with the composition of a single work, nay, it is mostly indulging in series of books which illustrate the intrinsic changeability of the chosen concept or contrast a work with another which once again deflects from the rectilinearity of creation. Thus the books cannot simply be separated as the literary part of D. R.'s work, for the books not only provide the space for texts, they also represent the widest area for elaborating on the pictures found, which follow one another page by page.

Even the first books, which were published in the fifties, are veritable machines for the production of pictures which go further as the imagination of the author would reach. The one called **kinderbuch** (childrens' book), whose simple geometric figurations, being easy and colourful to read are perforated by a number of various holes, is seemingly fixed in the optically seductive arrangement of the forms. However, every page only finds its face when the page behind it is considered and therefore reveals face after face when thumbing through the book. Moreover, the figurations are only valid in the context of the laws of reduction and symmetry, which govern the structure of the book. In the **bilderbuch** (picture book), the pages are arranged in a spring-clip folder, thus their sequence can be altered, – they consist of transparent, coloured foils which at that are also provided with rectangular holes. Here resources are already limited, only the most essential is used for purposes of differentiation, namely colours, some white separating sheets, occasional standardised perforations. However, the limitation is not just to be understood as an anticipation of efforts leading to **minimal art.** Despite the meticulous perfection resulting from it, the retreat to the scanty or sparing is connected with its meaning, it shows a desire to dispense with what is called phantasy, pictorial richness etc., in order instead to find a basis for the work on which by apparently simple reflections a different richness in significations can be developed. Thus the abandonment of the manifold, self-created forms also carries with itself the characteristics of the throwing away, stripping off, which later become more distinct in the shit books. However, they appear camouflaged in these first books, in a mask which D. R. was so successful in achieving at that time that for a long time it provided him with a face. In this range are of course also included the series of **books** which have been produced since 1958 and have formed his livelihood at certain times, thanks to their magnificence. They are portfolios of

18–24 loose sheets of coloured or black and white cardboard which are provided with various patterns of handcut slots. The book consists of the infinite possibilities of the variation which can be seen when the sheets are placed one on top of the other. Since the sheet is no longer aligned in one direction the methods of alteration branch on different levels: the sheets may be turned, changed in terms of sequence, and since they exist each in two colours (black-white, red-green etc.) they may be replaced by their complementary sheets. However, looking through the slots, which produces an optical excitation on the surface of the eye, is not only to be considered as a visual game. When we find in a diary note from 1966 the following: "looking through/as looking behind/looking forth/as looking in front", this indicates that an attempt is made in the **books** to formulate perception as the registration of different planes, one plane possibly acting on the other and justifying it without of course being able to separate itself independently. The looking through is also a trick which responds to the process of being seen, the shining through of something else on the surface of the outspread. The movement is answered by the countermovement, and the claim to transparency is suspended on the irridescent surface in front of which the gaze dwells. Also recognisable is the allusion to the problem of what lies behind and in front of the view, an abundance of attractions, a charming trap, which the eye digests or radiates.

From 1956–59 books were also produced from letters and other types published as **bok 1956–59** and as **ideograme** (ideograms). They are a discussion of the concepts and forms of **concrete poetry** propagated mainly by Eugen Gomringer, according to whose ideas the words should act directly in their visual or phonetic form, arranged in simple, clearly constructed systems, – as substance which carries meaning from the very beginning. D. R.'s commentary is an acceptance of what seems easily recognisable as style, the pursuance and deflection, before the trend becomes his own. He always leaves out what the ideogram perhaps made complete. The supposed quality of meaning of the word evaporates, since he often works with mere rudiments or arbitrary phonetic sequences which are then subjected to pictorial symmetry, which once again deprives them of their literal meaning. The words only appear as precisely set sequences of types, which achieve quality in their extremely complex relationships with type sequences on the same page or on previous or following pages, the position on the page, the alignment etc. being used as elements of the semantic constitution – a more extensive vocabulary, an imaginative grammar which can be varied from case to case. The printed pages are interrupted by unprinted black pages, which are also perforated in part, but here again only black appears, but not the same black. Other unprinted pages show only folds as markings or a crack. In addition **bok 1956 –59** dispenses with an established sequence of pages: in each book it is always different, only individual sequences are maintained, but instead of from front to back they may also be read from back to front, for the fixed polarity which determined the traditional book is replaced by the equivalence of the once established opposites.

One or two books appeared in quick succession in 1960–61 in **forlag ed** in Reykjavik, which D. R. himself had founded in order to publish not only his own works but also books by friends for whom he attended to the typography and equipment. The first books show the possibilities of the simplest vocabulary, i. e. in **bok 4 a,** two different triangular rubber clichés from which produced by repetition, displacement, overprinting etc. series of pictures take raise which are no longer easily recognisable and which can be continued arbitrarily. The series begins and ends at a point which does not provide a conclusive termination but is rather **one** outlet of a thought. **bok 3 a–d,** on the other hand, do not use exactly defined material nor even a material which is controlled in its variations, they are bound together at random from printed papers found by accident. Here too it is already shown how the books themselves begin to oppose to one another in their relationships which are constructed from simple symmetries, – what is the ease in **bok 1956–59** in one book, sets the pattern for publishing the entire work. For **bok 3 a** black and white sheets are bound from Icelandic daily newspapers, for **bok 3 c** coloured waste paper sheets from various printing houses. For **bok 3 b** sheets are bound from colourful comics which have been perforated several times; for **bok 3 d** sheets from black and white children's books which are also perforated several times. Using the few sets of opposites black and white – coloured, perforated – unperforated, relief printing – planographic printing (others can certainly be named), D. R. is able to instigate a simple game which does not enable the books to exist per se but already throws them to and fro in an endless reflection. The accumulation of the undefined printed matter continues the arrangements of **bok 4 a,** for they have proved that no solution could be represented as the correct one and that consequently any printed paper can take its place. The perforated books also lead the change which has so far been found in the limited field of meticulously selected papers and cleanly preserved cuttings into a kind of arbitrariness. They are a practice area for effects of change and depth which D. R. later uses at will in his pictures. On the other hand they show the grey pointlessness of the infinite permutation.

At the same time D. R. was producing books in the smallest sizes, which again contrast the miniature works with the large **boks,** and which do not allow the fixed idea to solidify into one version or vision. The **daily mirror book** uses the cut out pages of this English daily newspaper, which was selected because of its extremely contrasting layouts. **dagblegt bull** on the other hand parodies the past since it consists of coloured pieces of waste paper cut into small pieces. The small books, however, are not merely footnotes: the **daily mirror book** is continued in **quadratblatt** (quadrat print), a file of sheets which show huge enlargements of the small pages. The random collections of black areas or screen points now suddenly grow into significant graphics which one beside the other convey only fragments of legibility and do not permit any combination either – isolation of the book pages in the strictest sense without substituted autonomous meaning quantities. The **literaturwürste** (literature sausages) set a provisional settlement for these material books, sausages made from fat, spices and books and newspapers reduced to small pieces, products of turbid German post-war literature or the journalism accompanying it. The novels of Frisch and Grass contribute to the strength of the sausage, grey sacks on which the book cover shines as a label. The satire, which is particularly prominent here and directed towards a literature becoming noticeably more wretched and needy probably finds its culmination in those books appearing in 1975–76, the **Sammlung flachen Abfalls** (Collection of Flat Waste), a collection of 365 ring files, which include those flat objects which have gone through D. R.'s hands in one year, – an encyclopaedia of depreciation, which goes far beyond the narrow limits of satire and shows a possible end for the book production of D. R. But since the sausage has two ends the work as a whole cannot be put under one goal or motto, except if they both ended in the barking dog's mouth – well then the motto says: Bow-wow!

In 1960 D. R. received the prize of the **William and Noma Copley Foundation,** which at the same time enabled him to bring out a book at the expense of the foundation. The editor and technical advisor for these books was Richard Hamilton. D. R. corresponded with him, and in the letters the entire book was drafted from 1961–66; from Iceland, the USA and elsewhere Hamilton received printing copy and instructions for printing, some of which were very difficult to carry out since they were often only formulated in the form of hints to give the person printing the opportunity, or to force him to add his own interpretations. Due to the lengthy duration of its production the **(copley book)** – it bore no actual title – is a combination of the widest variety of visual, printed material, which is not bound but is only fastened together with a staple in a folder. However, these are not merely printed sheets, nay, the principle of printing is extended to blocking and punching. As daring as the purely technical efforts that required the technical expertise and inventiveness of the printers are the printed pictures. They are both devoid of pleasing smoothness that is ending in itself and of sobre, sketchy representation; they can hardly be described because they can never be separated from their representation, much more, they can only be found on the way from the find, the idea, to the transferring in the printing process on to a paper selected for this purpose. They comment on the method but always fluctuate between the simplicity which says precisely nothing and stays there and the infinite loop of self representation. The certainty of the process turns over into the uncertain as quickly as lightning, as D. R. decides instead of looking behind the process to include the way back and to look in front of it – instead of setting the picture and withdrawing, involving himself or trying both at the same time. Thus sheet by sheet can only or maybe also cannot be made accessible in the larger context of the work, what often appears so poor is the profoundly developed plan for the subsequent ejection of books and pictures, the sporadic notes for the deconstruction of the representation. And it must not be forgotten that this unique book owes its realisation to the devotion and effort of Richard Hamilton, who selflessly took upon himself the problems of mediating to produce the book.

A plan which is based on these outlines is perhaps the **MUNDUNCULUM**, which was published in 1967, the systematic application of the theories gained. The pictures in this book are produced from a series of stamps, apparently simple but ambiguous pictures. These can be given names, again according to position in relation to others, so that their coincidence in larger configurations at the same time permits a verbal interpretation, a beginning to a history yet to be told, which reads quite differently merely by turning the page. The interpretation is drawn from the pictures, is able to produce new pictures which can again be described. A machine which is quickly cranked up and which could in principle be able to grow pictures and texts ad infinitum if necessity wanted it, if the tracing of memory commanded it, which of course only forces to form pictures. If what is produced from this is its reply, and therefore represents some form of symmetry to it, this condition will perhaps indicate why the pictures tend so quickly, even in themselves, to provide themselves with a symmetrical axis – in **MUNDUN-CULUM** angels are symmetrical, the language is not their expression but their counterpart, to which they are indissolubly connected by their skin, and from which, however, they are impenetrably separated. In this connection **die blaue flut** (the blue tide) might also be mentioned, the diary of 1966, which was published in 1967 in a fine and proper typesetting. Blue is the memory which finds its complement in the present in the typographical translation into the book, memory, which in hand in the original form of notes and scribblings can be processed and serves as a fluctuating starting point for catching sight of the things to come, pattern and dotted screen through which something else could be seen.

In **POETRIE 1–5** (POESY 1–5), 1966–69, the extended book projects stretching over years begin. **POETRIE 1** (POESY 1) does indeed bear the subtitle **Halbjahresschrift für Poesie** (biannual review for poetry), but it never enters into the continuity of such a publication. This issue contains enigmatic pictures which in their privacy and in their provisional nature contrast with the purity of presentation in letter press. The majority of copies of the edition have been continued by hand by the author himself, the pictures therefore go one step further, go on wandering among the overlappings of colour, ascend to planes on which they make a brief halt and shine, and soon afterwards sink down again into the dim or solidify into black and white.

POETRIE 2 (POESY 2) contains clouds, short texts, researches and observations which do not cohere directly in terms of content but perhaps just in that they all embrace one concept or even several, enable it or them to become pictorial letting it or them go or become faint, – soft forms which slide into one another and hardly figured sail on and fade away. If the pictures in **POETRIE 1** spread and illustrate an outer strangeness, they perhaps find their reflection in the description of the inner strangeness in **POETRIE 2** – and hence slide into one another both inside and outside, relieve themselves of their metaphysical pretension when they are finally clapped on to the paper. **POETEREI 3–4** (POETING 3–4) contains two longer pieces of prose, major representations of the disillusioned turning about the objects or one's own body axis, just as automatically continuing efforts to approach the giddy heights. And as pictures for this an **Originalrhein** (Original Rhein), a section of the part of a postcard from Basle, which only shows the Rhein, a casually formed statement of the flowing, and an **Originalhammel** (Original Ram), a piece of cheese between the pages, which flat pressed and stinking transforms its mouldy colours. **POSIEREREI 5** (POESITIONING 5) is the partial translation of a novel by the Icelandic author Vigfús Björnsson, a transfer which follows the original text taking it literally throughout. The novel is then broken into pictures which appear to signify something and yet do not derive their excess of meaning from considered poetic intention but from the flat randomness of the literal understanding. A contrast to this is D. R's German contamination of Richard Hamilton's **Urban Image,** in which he follows the phonetic pattern of the words and chooses suitable German words for them.

In 1966 the volume of poems entitled **SCHEISSE** (SHIT) was published in Providence, since D. R. was then teaching at the Rhode Island School of Design, where together with the students he set and printed the book. The students had no knowledge of the German language and without technical ability introduced errors and defects into the pure collection of poems. Later more poems were added, which were finally all combined to form **DIE GESAMTE SCHEISSE** (COMPLETE SHIT), in 1968. This edition was reissued in a revised edition in 1973; this edition was again divided in 1974 into two revisions and from these were produced four volumes in 1975. This branching ends provisionally with these volumes. The shit poems have not been written down as a sequence of poems, they cannot be interpreted as a phase and hence expression of a specific, individual stability, from the beginning they are drifting objects, waste from the diaries, the work done on pictures, trips, stays and things found on them. When found together in the traditional form of a volume of poems, which again shows the traces of the intervening third party even in the first edition, the contradiction between (cumulative) unity and multiplicity/multiplication increases considerably in the course of this division, – much more, it falls into being hopelessly given up by to-and-fro-reflection. If the branching pretends to linearity and consistency, its resolution is found here in the simultaneity of the relationships, which apparently become closer, between parts which appeared to be for the most part the same and are now staged as being different in their respective places. The ramification should and will never take on a form, however, which would enable the elements of the series not yet present to be predicted, i. e. this form is not determined strictly by a law inherent in its development. Of course a concept can only be established according to rules which are accepted beforehand, but the system of rules itself is here integrated in the ramification, i. e. it is not only transitive but also reflexive. The bases themselves apparently turn into fluctuation and are included in the process of transformation. This is apparent in the changes seen in the poems: never the thought arises that the texts would be altered and deformed by a method that could be decoded and explained in time. In other words: the thought which would so easily arise in order to provide itself with definite categories of understanding of this process is rejected, for not the onedimensional reproduction of a scheme, not the repetition of serial mechanics, confirms itself, but the immediate breaking off, possibly even in the middle of the picture or text, shows the shrinking back from the examinable systematic proceeding. Repetition is necessary, however, in order to make a proceeding recognisable as such, but the moment of recognition of a proceeding is always taken away by the very change in direction. In form and style the shit poems are drawn from the inheritance of classical German poetry. In metrics and choice of words there is much which sounds of conceptual lyric poetry, via sayings to free rhythms, all digested with the trivial fringe material which penetrates, knocked down by rage, anxiety and sadness, which do not leave the measuredness on its safe path. The texts of a volume from 1974, for example, are only remnants of the first versions, so violently struck together that often only beginnings of lines remain, or lines enriched with consonants which interrupt their reading and leave it stuck in the rubbish. Even the list of contents has become a text, a flood of figures and title variations overgrows at once the index, which was once carefully arranged. The levelling of the wonderful, intruding heritage, the association with scrap, rubbish, waste and the thrown away, so that everything is converted and digested to complete shit, corresponds to the effort made to suspend the concentration on a sharply perceived centre and the rejection of the vague objects lying around in favour of a "general desharpening of focus" (D. R.) or of a thoroughgoing making distinct.

In addition to **die gesamte scheisse und ihre zweige** (the collected shit and its branches) a more modest family of books was published, namely **die tränenmeere und ihre verwandten** (the seas of tears and their relatives). This derives from D. R.'s idea to place a small advertisement in every edition of the Stadtanzeiger of Lucerne, short sentences, apparently with no meaning, which often formally resemble slogans, as are customary in these small town newspapers. The sentences vary from one edition to another, but only a little, often persist, become tautologies, which shortly afterwards are again negated, then begin at a different end. The privacy which gives rise to them, only makes sense in this environment, which marks it and to which it reacts by indicating in a gradual shift the purposeful, promising advertisement as likewise private nonsense, and therefore making it run into the void. This was so strikingly obvious that indignant readers demanded the end of the series of advertisements. The sentences have now been rescued in **Das TRÄNEN-MEER** (the Sea of Tears), 1973, a thick white book block without cover, where you merely thumb them through as they are standing one each on a single page until you reach the key point of publicity: "Fly Icelandair!" In addition to these pure variant, the original newspapers are bound together to form a huge grey pile called **der Tränensee** (the Lake of Tears). **Das TRÄNEN-MEER. BAND 2** (the Sea of Tears. Volume 2), which appeared shortly afterwards, puts opposite every sentence a drawing, a runoff which runs in a similar fashion to the sequence of the sentences – quietly, obstinately, openly offering their emptiness. As a result of the second printing, which the added pictures required, this volume became grey looking and unattractive. This would not be absolutely necessary, but it is consistent with the technique selected by D. R. of drawing directly on films or transparent papers which could be copied on to offset plates without the use of dotted screens and then be printed. This allows to be freely associated with dust and dirt, which may penetrate at any time and are just copied at will. The drawings remain the same in the third volume called **Dars Wähnen** (Sea of Tears 3), and to them are added new texts which refer to them, trying out many different interpretations, points of view, but referring back on themselves as soon as a starting point begins to shine through. Thus not abstract prose, which was itself quite sufficient, but a gliding from boundary to boundary, where language encounters what it can impossibly reach, i. e. the drawings which it is connected to. Written in the shortest possible time, the pieces endure for a long distance in the same place, giving nothing of themselves; dialogues replace what is required, they create a scene which in turn opens on to another scene,through which another scene can be recognised, on which the dialogue is paraphrased. The fourth volume, now being prepared, enlarges these essays to form a theatrical play, which is still being perfected with the greatest care. Beside the confusing shit ramification, the **tränenmeere** (seas of tears) are an easily definable shift from text to text + picture to picture + text etc., in which the same material must always assert itself in other combinings (the first text released from the newspaper against the unprinted pages), then approaches this point itself, finally to disappear – instead of the violent transformation of the shit poems, a minimal influencing of undefined conditions, a continuation of the experience to read a newspaper, the achievement of indifference in the soft exchange of the attained.

The **essays,** 1971–72, were firstly conceived as a second part to **MUNDUN-CULUM,** but whether they will be compiled in this sense is an open question. They do not constitute a vision, they ask questions which are directed to themselves, i. e. their purposefulness and the position of the person asking the questions conveyed in them. **2 PROBLEME UNSERER ZEIT** (2 problems of our time) provides the answer throughout the book, so that every page is filled with just one word – neatly placed in columns. All the pages together form one sentence, which standing off renounces and rejects both the expression of the clear and the unclear, except itself and the space it occupies in the book. **Ein Essay ÜBER DAS VERHALTEN DES ALLGEMEINEN ZU ODER GEGENÜBER DEM BESONDEREN BZW DES BESONDEREN ZU ORDER GEGENÜBER DEM ALLGEMEINEN** (An Essay ON THE RELATION OF THE GENERAL TO ORDER A SPECIAL OR THE GENERAL ORDERING A SPECIAL I. E. THE SPECIAL ORDERING A GENERAL) takes the question and its treatment even further in that a sentence, each letter of which is placed regularly one next to the other to fill one page, extends over hundreds of pages and denies that something should be said here, neither what has already been said nor the unsaid, a negation which cannot succeed if one wanted to consider it from the aspect of the goal, and which arbitrarily comes out into the open as a constant effort. Two other **essays** ask the questions **WER WAR MOZART** (Who was Mozart) and **WER IST DER DER NICHT WEISS WER MOZART WAR** (Who's the one who does not know who Mozart was) in their titles, which are briefly answered both times by: "Ich weiss es nicht" ("I do not know"). Since there is basically nothing to say except the conceit that here and now this or that must be expressed what one does not know or what feigns itself to be knowledge, every sentence becomes a ridiculous farce, a play or a lie which automatically stops when the "don't know" is confirmed. For even this manages to fill a book if correctly inserted or extended over the pages by typesetting, – the publication, even if it tended to contract into gestures or mere statement, still carries the blame with itself for making a claim which it cannot honour under any circumstances, unless it was naïve.

In addition to these field excursions into the area of the sciences of man, D. R. moves into popular literature when he decides to write popular novels himself, the **Bastel-Novellen,** 1974–75. They are equivalent to their predecessors, in their colourful appearance with the worst advertisements – the text uses fragments from trivial literature, which constantly break up and are shipwrecked, just as this steamer on a raging sea, endlessly portraying itself rocking through the first story, by the old method of one picture in another, which in turn shows the same picture, and so on into infinity. The unsaid, inconceivable, dwells on this point, which D. R.'s writing constantly approaches and the very picture of which it is or rather becomes, since it never reaches this point, whether dozens follow the first two novels published. Perhaps this could explain the fact that any book series can be interrupted at any point and does not necessarily serve as constraint for production – but the breaking off in the middle of one's stride or the abandonment of toilsome effort is a new departure which the picture needs to succeed.

To avoid giving preference to any of the works mentioned D. R. has been engaged in publishing **gesammelte werke** (collected works) since 1969 in the

edition hansjörg mayer, in which he was a partner from 1968 to 1977, an undertaking whose 1st part was completed last year with 20 volumes. The work of D. R. is reproduced here book by book, reconstructed or even partially enlarged, an edition, however, which is not at an end but which will continue into the future. These volumes, however, are not merely a re-issue of the books out of print, they must be read differently, each one of them, as they are interpretations of the present. Thus they have no uniform configuration either, only the typography of Hansjörg Mayer, to whose inestimable services it must be ascribed that such an edition was made possible – which other German publishers would have been ready for it at that time of nostalgia – gives the volumes the cohesion which they conceal to a greater or lesser extent by their colourfulness and confusing montages. The second part of **gesammelte werke** will cover the books that have appeared since 1971, the reflected is approaching closer and closer to the reflecting, since the temporal distance between the two is constantly being reduced. The fact that the point where the original and the second edition appear at the same moment would be the point of identity where the reflection would end and where the lake would dry up, where nothing more would be said nor concealed, doubtlessly does not come into question – the volumes to come merely admit that they are indispensable anyway, be it only in the imagination.

III

"I am a pane of glass in the palace of glass, I do not separate anything. In front there is nothing to see. Behind there is nothing to see either. The blind man knows the credulity of the light."
Danielle Sarréra, **L'Ostiaque**

D. R.'s pictures, beside the many-sided versatile books, are not the confirmation of an interpretation, the fine goal of creation, the valid clean copies that are expected from masterpieces, unless they are followed into their poverty and what is negative in them is found as the conceived positive. The pictures sweep what is flaking off to the front or show a sweet, slippery smoothnes, a provocatively stupid simplicity or an infatuatingly irridescent, decaying passing away.

Most closely associated with the books are of course the graphics since they also consist in the dizzy and swindling reflective interplay between printing plates and paper prints. It would therefore be erroneous to assume that they represent a simple reproduction technique whose dominant feature is quantity. Certainly this must not be suppressed, for it is the assurance that the picture will powerfully assert itself, even though presenting itself scantily and miserably before the publisher and the public as an individual item. However, the fact that as printed matter it has achieved a new quality, that first of all it is simply good, follows from the fact that it always has a double, a symmetrical double, and therefore does not offer an exposed surface of attack but reduces its impression and expression to zero. This position of rest is temporarily deceptive, but new printing processes, new colours are always being raised up, only to repress and to switch off the accumulated mass of significance again and again. In the coloration two movements can be observed: one picture can be resolved in numerous layers which in turn are based merely on one decision, the discretion of the author with himself. The colours are interchangeable, their function is a constructive one, namely that of distinction, they have no properties, do not represent any deviations from natural laws. This is shown in the fact that they can be changed during the printing process, that they are mixed only on the rollers or find their goal being continually remixed. This goal would be the calling to attention or veiling of one layer – the unique prints which are produced in the movements or transpositions mentioned, show the varying distinctness of the predetermined colour separations (which, for example, can even be made mechanically) emerging from the mutual relations between them. The other possibility of producing colour would be this: a single picture in one colour is given several upper layers of other colours which never adhere to the set theme but seek to shift it, which make up for gaps or produce new ones, heighten the picture. The picture that is finally obtained is therefore based not on components formed in it from the beginning but seeks to bring together the components which are intended to outbid or to stun each other to gabby silence. In D. R.'s earliest graphic attempts, in which colour is scarcely handled, he replaces their alternation with the multiple, shifted use of the single printing form which makes the picture once formed with clear contour into flickering. Another method is to replace the colours with chocolate, bananas, biscuits which are pressed from the copper plate or squashed on to the paper. The colours then finally escape control, and often they only emerge truly at a later date when the materials have begun to decompose. One go opens up a multitude of colours and shapes, for the squeezed material easily surpasses the depths prescribed for it by the etched plate, with its markings. In addition nothing serves better to indicate that it is the invisible axis between the model and the copy that is being represented than the speed with which the pressing is done, which in the space of a moment has reduced the world to nothing and always leaves behind on the sheet only the residues of sadness. What the graphics show, and what on them starts off on the journey into the world and its understanding is therefore the misprinted colour remnant on the paper, which points to the uncertain, on the one hand, and the multitude of immense forms on the other, which take off for the unreadable or are rescued just in time by the simple tricks of the recognisable faces or the cats' heads used.

In close association with the graphics can be found further inventions for making pictures mechanically, such as the stencils through which arbitrary colours and materials can be spread, or the stamps which form an arsenal which brings into play given meanings in a multitude of different ways which cannot be caught up linguistically. These basic forms, which are so impressive, that they appear to be sufficient to bring the world to its common denominator, assert themselves through countless pictures, – particularly the motor cyclist whose silhouette is able to change into heart or ass struggles remotely and shadowlike through the mishaps which befall him in the moulding of the chocolate or the rotting waste, or appears as a schematic phantom that has suddenly shown up out of insignificant trifles. This continued going on appears to be one of the most important qualities of the pictures and drawings at all. Continued going on means the inclusion of the widest variety of means of representation in the writing of an expression. Since the identity of the expressed object is even lost in one sentence in the distance between beginning and end, since it is afflicted by the incalculability of what penetrates speech, whose obtrusiveness cannot be corrected by the frame, there is no other way out but to abandon the initial intention. What is brought to an end is driven off to other shores or run aground somewhere on the deposited sand. The large piles of mould or the islands of cheese and yoghurt leave aside these impulses to expression and put in their place the unpleasant and the repulsive so that they form a monument which turns into the stylising of these resistances. The charms obtained from the multicoloured interchange of stinking piles is then countered by D. R. when he employs the peace of the banal, the rippling quality of the huge boxes full of piled up masses of spices. All these sagged qualities, the softness of the small glaring red cheeses, which are crawling with maggots, the hollow mixture of odours from the spices, the sweet joyfulness of the chocolate lions, the trash which sentimentally radiated by the thick, colourful drops of paint over the pictures or by the toy planes or figurines stuck in the mud, are pushed separately to the front to contrast with the blameless highly esteemed. The continued going on, which would not care a jot about what in the world as a carrier of predetermined significance opposes to it, must lose its way in the trap of style – whether this be masterly or merely a trivial attitude. What D. R. is able to achieve on the contrary, is the unfolding of bounding ideas, he does not walk in between them but rather falls below them, draws his way from one to the other, at whose border a glimpse occasionally occurs. The features of separate letters, which often present themselves sporadically in the thicket of the lines, and – standing indeed on different planes of the picture – appear as if they might be able to be read together in one unit, are always only fragments, however, which never form themselves into one perception unless to enable us to see their fragmentation. To be seen is therefore only a sequence of places which arises from time to time in our vision and even claims its reversal. The places form the values which a consideration of the picture presents, they establish themselves impossible for simultaneous perception because of their disparity, the bridges which are thrown to them signify the attempt at resolution which eventually denies itself the picture, the desire to clear up with oneself and the picture. The pictures and the host of pencil drawings that have been produced in recent years are therefore always self portraits, what they are often called even when they seek to feature the author as a fragmentary piece of his work. Thus the fact that the theme of the picture is constantly shifting – one picture must follow the other to catch up with what has gone before, what has been lost – the fact that the pictorial is added to the temporal displacement, which rejects the subject from the solid centre to the background or the foreground, also gives rise to other properties such as the brush stroke which is no longer covered up and thus to assert its content. The picture never allows its surface to be forgotten, its careless treatment stops perception, and attention is drawn to it since in fact it is just as much a trace of the author as his vague, glimmering portrait. However, the pictures do not simply end up on the side of chaos, the thoroughgoing audacity of abandonment which they perhaps would like to achieve. Again and again they are traversed by simple constructions which are often disguised as a window, promising a glimpse through or a view out, where a new scene opens up. Not one scene, nay, the window splits open the vision, permits a view in four window sections which are slightly reminiscent of the desire to keep the untamed One under the spell, at least by its reflection. This reflection, however, finds its counterpart in the other window half – it can no longer be decided now which picture is the first, the reflection or its scheme, the sobre pattern of division, retains the upper hand. The window glass is not capable of anything else but to throw the picture back to the observer.

Biographie

Dieter Roth

1930 born in hanover
mother german   father swiss

1936 primary school hanover-döhren
1940 secondary school hanover

1943 moves to switzerland
accomodated by fritz wyss   zurich
classical secondary school
drawings   pastels
poems

1946 parents move to switzerland
lives with them in herisau
classical secondary school   st gallen
etching (on tin sheet metal)
oil paintings

1947 bellach
grafic design apprentice at studio
friedrich wüthrich   bern   (til 1951)
first lino- and woodcuts
meets franz eggenschwiler and paul talman

1949 gerlafingen
collages (painted scrap metal)

1950 privat lessons in lithography by
eugen jordi   kehrsatz
tries without success to refuse military service

1951 odd jobs on building sites
watercolours
meets marcel wyss and eugen gomringer
foundation of review 'spirale'

1952 cleaning of the jesuit church in solothurn
unique prints (ex libris 'franz')
refuses military service successfully
dismissal from the army

1953 bern
odd jobs   decorations
graphic design for exhibitions
first issue of 'spirale' published
meets daniel spoerri   claus bremer
peter althaus

1954 first baked sculpture (spiral   made of dough
in a shop window)
experiments in op-art
(screens   complementary contrast
reflected light   deflected light)
ladder (open air sculpture exhibition   biel)
first book with holes 'childrens book'
(published 1957)
first film   light and shadow on the stairs
of the bubenbergrain

running of gallery 33 together with
rolf iseli   peter meier and walter vögeli
(permanent exhibition by the group)
kiefer-hablitzel award for painting

1955 graphic design
invited to copenhagen by percy v. halling-koch
designer for 'unika-vaev'

1956 copenhagen
textil design
ideograms (published 1959)
films   1) out of the rear window of a tram
2) in a football stadium   swinging the
camera with a piece of string around the head
3) black film with holes
meets gerhard rühm

1957 reykjavík
married to sigríður björnsdóttir
work with a goldsmith
coloured drawings with compass and pen
screen prints
foundation 'forlag ed' (with einar bragi)
publication of books by both authors
son karl born

1958 work for architects
work on books with slots (published 1959)
colour films   1) single frame shots
2) made with 12 circles of various sizes
work for 'material 1' (published 1959)
contribution to 'neues forum'
invited to philadelphia by the architect
newcomb montgomery

1959 new york
graphic designer at geigy corp.
visiting critic at yale university
work on 'bok 2' and 'bok 4'
(published 1960–1961)
meets norman ives

may reykjavík
kinetic pictures (puzzles)
geometric rubberstamp pictures
kinetic sculptures
publication of a book by sigríður björnsdóttir

1960 work at ragnar kjartansson's
ceramics workshop
books of unique prints (using one printing
forme only)
photograms
pictures made with halftone screens
contributions to   'concrete poetry'   'nota'

july copenhagen
exhibition of books at addi koepcke's gallery

aug. basle
work at the advertising agency
of karl gerstner and markus kutter
publication of a book by paul talman
meets emmett williams and jean tinguely

nov. paris
festival d'art d'avantgarde
(kinetic pictures and filmprojections
on moving mirrors)
meets robert filliou

dec. william and noma copley foundation award

1961 reykjavík
making of architectural models
(with magnús pálsson)
work on a book for the copley foundation
via correspondence with richard hamilton
collages of texts
manuscript with holes

march amsterdam
exhibition 'bewogen beweging'
(poster with holes)
books made out of run-up sheets
and newspapers
the 'literature sausage'
dumb pictures ('stupidograms')
textfilm (a letter)
contribution to 'kalenderrolle 1'
article about d. rot by richard hamilton
in 'typographica 3'
publication of a book by alcopley
son björn born

1962 reykjavík
work on 'mundunculum' (published 1967)
picture alphabet (23 rubberstamps)
conjugations
kinetic objects (rotation- and sound-
pictures)
contributions to 'kalenderrolle 2'
'daily bul'

1963 newspaper illustrations
the negative image (flake-off pictures
mould-pictures kitsch-pictures)
contributions to 'kalender 63' 'v tre'
'an anthology'
work for 'edition originär'
(published 1965)
illustrations for '4 leikbaettir' by
oddur björnsson
daughter vera born

1964 stencilbox for do-it-yourself pictures
(with paint shoe-polish nail-varnish etc)

aug. stays with arnold saks in new york

sept. philadelphia
work on 'snow' at the museum college of art
indistinct images ('faints')
meets alison knowles dick higgins
charlotte moorman nam june paik
george brecht al hansen bob watts
joe jones in new york

nov. new haven
teaching at yale university
(school of architecture)
screen prints with chocolate
screen prints with additions

1965 providence
teaching at rhode island school of design
non-teaching as teaching
poems for 'scheisse' (published 1966)
soundalphabet (for playing texts)
decomposition-pictures and -objects
(symbol-figures)
pressings and squashings as graphics
etchings with chocolates bananas
biscuits etc
contributions to 'kalender 65' 'integration'
'spatial poem 1' by chieko shiomi
translation of the french part of
daniel spoerri's 'topography'
work for 'poetry 1' (published 1966)
meets andré thomkins
work with rudolf rieser

1966 alteration of texts by others
correction of texts by others
name of a print as print
numbering stamp with 10 images
diaries and address books as lists of ideas
negative pin-ups
illustrated books as pieces of music
fading pictures (and their opposites)
meets oswald wiener

june markgröningen
work on 'die blaue flut'
contributions to 'et 2' 'joglars'
'frau und fräulein' 'gorgona'
'spatial poem 2' by chieko shiomi
'blockprint' 'le petit colosse de simi'
during the summer the studio is cleared out
by the houseowner all objects and pictures
are destroyed
work on '246 little clouds' (published 1968)

1967 reykjavík
work on 'poetrie 2' (published 1967)
'die blaue flut 2'
2 alphabets for computer
colouring book for children
colouring sheet for adults
work on double book 'noch mehr scheisse'
and 'footnotes to sweethearts . . .'
(with emmett williams)
lives with dorothy iannone

sept. basle
120 mould heaps
handpainted books
books with filled pages
contribution to 'décollage'

1968 london
teaching at watford school of art
recipe for a book without theme
(carried out by students)
the unpleasant embarassing and weak diary
printing of the review (10 copies)
melancholic nippets (cats and gnomes
stuck in chocolate)
translation of '14 chansons' by robert filliou

may düsseldorf
teaching at the art academy
selfportraits made out of edibles
(as old man corpse dog etc)
maggot- and flycolonies
soft sculptures (cheese meat)
the studio at the academy is cleared out by
unknown persons
joins edition hansjörg mayer
publication of the collected works
work with hartmut kaminski

july reykjavík
translation of the english part of
daniel spoerri's 'topography'
(with own additions)
contributions to 'ica bulletin'
'zeitkunst im haushalt'

1969 düsseldorf
pictures with spices

may hidden rot (40 suitcases filled with cheese
at gallery eugenia butler los angeles)

idea sound and props for 2 films
(part of maurizio kagel's 'ludwig van')

july reykjavík
work on a serialised novel (free version
of the story '2 tvöfaldir & 4 einfaldir'
by vigfús björnsson)
(the first instalments published 1969 and 1971)
takes down his part of the exhibition 'freunde'
before the opening (kunsthalle bern)
contributions to 'daily bul'
'pop architecture' 'interfunktionen 3'
work with the petersburg press

1970 düsseldorf
citysights (screenprints)
banal-romantic monumentalism
(large containers with wasting and
rotting stuff)
franz lehar's sofatext
cashregister texts (with stefan wewerka)
urban mud (transplantation of a text by
richard hamilton)

collaborations with stefan wewerka
(cologne stuttgart braunschweig berlin
munich reykjavík)
work with karl egon schulz

1971 reykjavík london düsseldorf braunschweig
berlin luzern
poems for 'eine nachlese'
work in progress 1) 2 sentences a week
as advertisments (luzerner stadtanzeiger)
2) one lithograph a week from
the same stone (petersburg press)
essays
preparation of a travelling exhibition
of books and graphics
(with hansjörg mayer and hanns sohm)

1972 Reykjavík, Stuttgart, Braunschweig, Berlin,
London, Zürich, Düsseldorf, Wien
breaking down the drive of perspective
(Berlin Scenes)
starts the Seas of Tears
Poetry Workshop No. 1 with Achleitner, Brus,
Rühm, Wiener (Berlin)
the exhibition of books and graphics starts
travelling from the Gemeente Museum,
Den Haag
exhibition of announcements of
'Pictures Made to Order'
(Gallery Grünangergasse, Wien)

1973 Zug, Reykjavík, Hellnar, Stuttgart, Braunschweig, Berlin, London, Zürich, Hamburg,
Luzern, Wien
1st Collection of 'Flat Waste'
collotype prints
ridiculous jewellery
(at Langenbacher & Wankmiller, Luzern)
'Rarely Heard Music', with Rühm and Wiener
(verbalising about a piece of music within
that piece)
collaboration with Arnulf Rainer (Wien)
branching of a book ('The Complete Shit')

1974 Hamburg, Hellnar, Braunschweig, Berlin,
Luzern, Zug, Zürich, Reykjavík, Wien, Watford,
München, Stuttgart
appearance of the shit-style in pictures
(timidly)
first almost perfect shit-poem
trying to depict the world as ego (diaries)
stage play out of one word ('Murmel')
lifting of the appearance of pictures, with
titles and tits
founded 'Dieter Roth's Familien Verlag' and
'Dieter Roth Pictures, Zug'
'Rarely Heard Music' with Attersee, Brus,
Nitsch, Rainer, Rühm, Wiener at Berlin
work with Arnulf Rainer

1975 Braunschweig, Hamburg, Hellnar, Mosfellssveit, Stuttgart, Diessen, Berlin, Wien,
London, Watford, Karlsruhe, Zug, Luzern,
Vornbach, Zürich
shit-music (piano)
founded 'Review for everything'
(edition hansjörg mayer)
a stageplay for the inner voices
(Sea of Tears, No. 4)
video work with Arnulf Rainer
Exhibition of notes and scetches
(Gallery Kurt Kalb, Wien)
'Rarely Heard Music' with Brus, Nitsch,
Rühm (Wiener), 'the Karlsruhe Concert'
and 'String-quartett'

1976 Akureyri, Mosfellssveit, Hellnar, London,
Watford, Cadaqués, Barcelona, Stuttgart,
Hamburg, Diessen, Braunschweig, Vornbach,
Wien, Zug, Reggio d'Emilia, Cavriago,
Solothurn
'certified paintings' with Richard Hamilton
and 'Hundelieder', with Chispas Luis and
Richard Hamilton, at Cadaqués
telephone-doodles
'Letter-forms', with Arnulf Rainer
Discussions as 'Lieder'. with Oswald Wiener
expanding autobiography
second 'Flat Junk'-collection
developing stories out of pictures (from an
exhibition with Richard Hamilton)

1977 Aarau, Barcelona, Basel, Berlin, Braun-
schweig-Oelper, Cadaqués, Chicago,
Den Haag, Düsseldorf, Erlangen, Hamburg,
Hellnar, Kopenhagen, Lausanne, Lodmunda-
fjord, London, Luzern, Madrid, Markgröningen,
Mosfellssveit, New York, Prinzendorf,
Reykjavík, Stuttgart, Wien, Zug
The 'Quadrupelkonzert', at the
Music Academy of Basel
work with Richard Hamilton
work with Arnulf Rainer
changed 'Dieter Roth's Familien Verlag' into
'Dieter Roth's Verlag'
recording dogs' barking at Mount Tibidabo,
Barcelona
work with George Brecht, Richard Hamilton
and Stefan Wewerka
first piece of negative music
(Scheisse in music) as piano-sonata
work on 'the collected sonnets'

Selected One-man Shows: 1958 Mokka Kaffi, Reykjavík
1960 Galerie Koepcke (with Christian Megert), Kopenhagen
1963 Galerie Koepcke, Kopenhagen
1964 Museum School of Art, Philadelphia
1967 Galerie Zwirner (with Dorothy Ionnone), Köln
Galerie der edition hansjörg mayer, Stuttgart
1968 Galerie Zwirner, Köln
Galerie Block, Berlin
Galerie Tobies & Silex (with Stefan Wewerka), Köln
1969 Galerie Ernst, Hannover
Galerie Eugenia Butler, Los Angeles
Galerie Müller, Stuttgart
1970 Galerie Werner, Köln
Galerie Mikro (with Stefan Wewerka), Berlin
1971 Galerie Toni Gerber, Bern
Eat Art Galerie, Düsseldorf
Museum Haus Lange, Krefeld
1972 Gemeentemuseum, Den Haag
Galerie Grünangergasse, Wien
1973 Hayward Gallery, London
Kunsthalle, Basel
Helmhaus, Zürich
The Vancouver Art Gallery, Vancouver
Galerie Steinmetz, Bonn
1974 Kestner Gesellschaft, Hannover
Kunstverein Hamburg
1975 Stedelijk Museum Amsterdam
Galerie Grünangergasse, Wien
1976 Galerie Kurt Kalb, Wien
Galerie Cadaqués (with Richard Hamilton) Cadaqués
1975 Stedelijk Museum Amsterdam
Galerie Ziegler, Zürich
Galerie Grünangergasse, Wien
Dieter Roth Pictures, Hamburg
1976 Galerie Kurt Kalb, Wien
Museum Solothurn
(with Richard Hamilton:)
Galeria Cadaqués, Cadaqués
British Counsel Inst., Barcelona
Turnpike Gallery, Leigh
Dieter Roth Pictures, Hamburg
1977 (with Richard Hamilton:)
ICA, London
Kunsthaus, Aarau
Gemeente Museum, Den Haag
Junior Galerie, Düsseldorf
Fondacion Miró, Barcelona
Galerie EUDE, Barcelona
(with Björn and Karl Roth:)
Galeria Cadaqués, Cadaqués
Galerie Handschin, Basel
Galerie Stähli, Zürich
Langenbacher & Wankmiller, Luzern
Galerie AELE, Madrid
Dieter Roth Pictures, Hamburg

Selected Group-shows:

1953 'Berner Künstler' Galerie Schindler, Bern
1954 Permanente Ausstellung, Galerie 33, Bern
     'Plastik im Freien', Biel
1955 'Junge Berner Künstler', Kunsthalle, Bern
1957 'Die Zeichnung im Schaffen jüngerer Schweizer Maler und Bildhauer', Kunsthalle, Bern
1959 'Motion in Vision-Vision in Motion', Hessenhuis, Antwerpen
     'Dynamo Zero', Galerie Boukes, Wiesbaden
     'Edition MAT', Société d'Art Saint Germain des Prés' Paris
1960 'Oeuvres d'Art Transformable' Gallery One, London
     'Festival d'Art d'Avantgarde', Paris
1961 'Bewogen Beweging', Stedelijk Museum, Amsterdam
     'Nove Tendencije 1', Galerija Suvremene Umjetnosti, Zagreb
1962 'Myndlistaskólinn Reykjavíkur', Asmundarsalur, Reykjavík
1963 'Schrift en Beeld', Stedelijk Museum, Amsterdam
1964 'Edition MAT Coll 64', Galerie der Spiegel, Köln
1965 '100 Artists', PVI Gallery, New York
     'Artists Key Club', American Theatre for Poets, New York
     'Between Poetry and Painting', ICA London
     'A new concept in art galleries', Multiples Inc., New York
1966 'Recent Still Life', Museum of Art, Providence
     'Object Poems', Something Else Gallery, New York
     'Toward more sensible Boredom', Filmmakers Cinematheque, New York
1967 'Fetische', Galerie Tobies & Silex, Köln
1968 'Sammlung Hahn', Wallraf-Richartz Museum, Köln
     'Graphik und Objekte', Documents IV, Kassel
     'Edition Hansjörg Mayer', Gemeentemuseum Den Haag
1969 'Concrete Poetry', Fine Arts Gallery University of British Columbia, Vancouver
     'Freunde + Freunde', Kunsthalle Bern
     '3. Biennale der Ostseestaaten', Kunsthalle, Rostock
     'Súm III', Galerie Súm, Reykjavík
1970 'Damenfrisör', Düsseldorf
     'Das Ding als Objekt', Kunsthalle, Nürnberg
     'Postkarten', Kunstmuseum, Luzern
     'Beethoven 1770–1970', Neue Galerie, Aachen,
1971 'Schweizer Zeichnungen im 20. Jahrhundert', Staatliche Graphische Sammlung, München
     'Multiples the first decade', Museum of Art, Philadelphia
1972 'Amsterdam–Paris–Düsseldorf', Guggenheim Museum, New York
     'Giovane Arte Svizzera', Comune di Milano, Milano
     '8th International biennal exhibition of prints', Tokyo
1973 'Mit Kunst leben', Württembergischer Kunstverein, Stuttgart
     '6. Internationale Triennale für farbige Druckgraphik', Haldenschulhaus, Grenchen
1974 'Artists Books', University Art Museum, Berkeley
     'Artists Stamps', Simon Fraser Gallery, Burnaby
1976 '20 Jahre Museum Haus Lange', Krefeld
     'Gemeinschaftsarbeiten', Galerie Wiener und Würthle, Berlin
     (mit Attersee, Brus, Nitsch, Rühm, Steiger, Wiener)
     'Schweizer Zeichnungen', Kunsthaus, Zürich
1977 Bücher und Zeichnungen, Dokumenta VI, Kassel